HACKAMORE REINSMAN

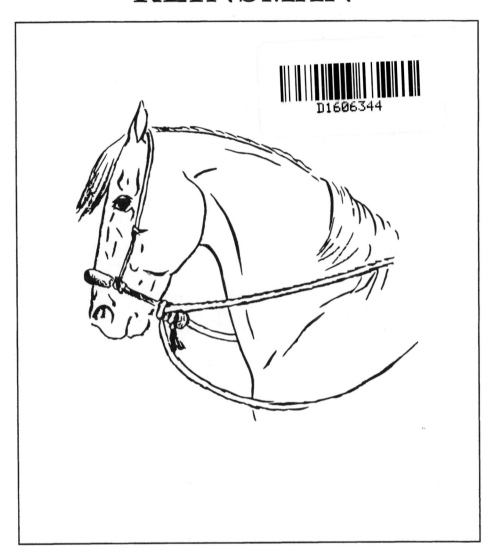

BY ED CONNELL
ILLUSTRATED BY RANDY STEFFEN

LENNOCHE PUBLISHERS
WIMBERLEY, TEXAS

First Printing January, 1952
Twentieth Printing, April 2002

To place orders for *Hackamore Reinsman,* contact:
Leslee Connell Schwartz
Lennoche Publishers
201 Windmill Cove
Wimberley, Texas 78676
(512) 847-3399
Fax: (512) 847-6819
www. hackamore-reinsman.com

Printed in the United States
Sheridan Books, Inc.
100 North Staebler Road
Ann Arbor, Michigan 48103

TABLE OF CONTENTS

Page

FOREWORD

The flashy, turn-at-a-touch bridle horses of the ancient **Californios** have always been admired by horsemen in every part of the United States. Many an old-timer Texan, fresh from the **brasada** of his home range, stood back and silently admired the maneuverability of the California cow horses at the end of the long cattle drive from Texas to the sunny land of the Pacific. While he probably didn't approve of the spade bits in the mouths of these **caballos**, he grudgingly had to admit to himself that the mounts of the dark skinned **vaqueros** could throw themselves around after a cow!

California was a land of **mañana** ... the cowboys of the **Dons** took many more pains, and much more time in the training of their bridle horses than the bowlegged knight of the Texas brush country ever dreamed of spending on the Spanish ponies that helped trail the herds of Texas cattle to the grassy slopes of the Pacific. But he did admire the results, and would have been proud to own such a mount!

The details of training the California bridle horse with the Spanish **jaquima** (hackamore), have been a trade secret with the descendants of the **vaqueros** for many years. Their methods were passed on from father to son, and from friend to close friend ... always by word of mouth. Nothing was ever written about the fine points of the art, and as a result there are probably less than a score of men in California today who actually **understand** and **practice** the art of the ancient **vaqueros**!

During the last two or three years several books have been written on the hackamore, but these works have confined themselves mostly to instructions to the craftsman on **how** to make a hackamore from the raw materials, but very little on how to use it. To my knowledge, this is the first work to lift the veil of secrecy from the methods necessary to make a hackamore horse ... from start to the stage where he's ready for the bridle, according to the high standards of old-time **Californios**.

Written by a man whose name has been very little in the limelight of horse circles, for his life has been spent **doing** the things so many spend their lives **talking** about, this book is an authentic manual of instruction that will enable the serious horseman to train his colts with the methods of the HACKAMORE REINSMAN, an almost extinct species of man!

1

This writer had the pleasure and privilege of working with Ed Connell, the author of this book, for a long enough period of time to be thoroughly convinced that he knew exactly what he was talking about, and that he practiced what he preached ... with results! Considering the age-old differences of opinion between the two schools of the cowman ... the Texas way, and the California way, it may seem strange to many that a Texan should advocate methods of the **vaquero** ... should abandon the snaffle and grazing bit for the hackamore and the ... spade bit, you ask? Well, no ... every man to his own preferences when it comes to bits for the finished horse. The **good** horsemen among the California spade bit men are **good**, and do wonders with the big old spoon. But that's the beauty of hackamore training ... when the hackamore horse is ready for the bridle, he can be worked with any kind of a curb bit, for he's already learned to handle himself in the hackamore, and the bit is merely another means of doing exactly what was done with the rawhide nose-band and rein-knot.

There's no doubt that there are other methods that will make just as well-reined a horse as the hackamore way ... and perhaps some of them in less time ... BUT...if you want to learn the ways of the California reinsman...digest every word of this book...their knowledge and skill will be yours for the taking!

Now a word about the author ... then you can get on with the part I know you're so anxious to dive into! Ed Connell is a native of the Golden State, and has had his legs over a horse right from the beginning of his life. He's got enough age on him that he worked with the old-time big California spreads, breaking colts and making bridle horses for the vast **remudas** of spreads like Miller & Lux, and others of like-caliber. He was lucky in having old-time **vaqueros** take a shine to him, and impart their knowledge of the hackamore and its use to his eager mind. In all my ramming around the horse country, I've never run into a more serious, or able horseman. Unlike the close-mouthed old-timers he learned from, Ed Connell has a burning desire to pass his rare knowledge on to the generations of future horsemen...and posterity. In his determination to prevent the use of the hackamore from becoming a lost art, the author has labored over this manuscript for several years. Even now he is working on another that takes up the use of the bridle ... where this one stops.

2

Now before handing you the reins of your horse, let me stress one fact. This is not a book for entertaining reading. It's a manual of instruction, and only that. To get anything out of it you'll have to study every word and every picture ... not just once, but many times. To many of you the methods stressed here will come no easier than your first lesson in solid geometry, or your first semester of Latin! But it's here ... pursue it diligently enough, and the knowledge will be yours!

May you always ride a good horse!

RANDY STEFFEN

About the Author
EDGAR N. CONNELL

Ed Connell was born on July 28, 1900 in Livermore, California. He came from a highly educated family, but an educated life did not interest him. He knew what he wanted to do and at the age of seventeen, he left home to work on a cattle ranch. His parents let him go thinking he would be back to school again soon. When he didn't return he became the black sheep of the family for years.

His first job was with John Moy running cattle at the Floyd Camp. Ed started out as all boys of that age did, with chores like chopping wood for the cook and riding in between times. In 1918, he was with the Moy cattle ranch when the rodeo was held several miles north of Livermore at the Anderson ranch. This was about the time the rodeo circuit, as we know it now, started. Ed rode three bulls that day and managed to stay on top. He remembered being well pleased with himself.

The next year Ed went to work for Jimmy Moy, who was running cattle in the Mocho Creek area, Cedar Mountain and the Devil's Hole country. By this time he was riding colts and learning all he could about making a reined horse. He had good teachers, men that knew the business. His next job was starting colts with Lee Ogier in the Mount Hamilton area. In those days the horses and cattle were handled and worked together. As soon as a horse was started he was used with the cattle.

Ed broke horses and cowboyed for practically all the cattle ranches in the Mount Hamilton district: the Gerber ranch, Hubbards, Morrows, Orestimba, Oak Flat and the Canada out of Gilroy. He started horses for Firebaugh and the Miller & Lux Bloomfield ranch. Ed also worked the great Hearst ranch on the King City side. At that time a starting job was generally a 30 or 40 day job; there was always another one waiting.

By this time Ed had become an accomplished horseman and cattleman. He came back to the Livermore area and went to work for D. M. McLemore. There were no trucks in those days, and wherever cattle had to be moved they were driven over the roads. McLemore bought and sold thousands of cattle from all over the west. Ed became his head shipper on the railroad with headquarters in Barstow. The Barstow cattle yards were well-kept and big. Train loads of cattle would come in, and Ed would classify them and send them out.

Then the depression hit, and countless people went broke including McLemore. There was no work to be found as the ranchers had no money to pay for the help they needed. The Hetch Hetchy miners were about the only people working. They spent their money freely on the week-ends giving the cowboys a chance to part with their earnings by playing poker. Ed became a very good poker player.

About that time, Ed's father came looking for him and convinced Ed to return to school. He went to the University of California at Davis and took a two year non-degree course in animal husbandry. When he finished, Ed went back to working with horses and cattle.

For some time, Ed worked with the H. Moffat Company in the San Joaquin Valley. Moffat was one of the biggest cattle outfits in the west. Ed also cowboyed in Nevada and southeast Oregon. This was big country with few fences. A rider could go from Elko County, Nevada into Idaho without going across a fence.

It was at this time that Ed began to think about writing a book on the training of the California reined horse. No one had, and it was needed to keep the method from dying out. Ed knew the system thoroughly and was one of the few who did.

It took him two and a half years to write the first half of the method, the book on hackamore training. It was 1946. The manuscript was sent to a dozen or two publishers in California. All of them turned it down. A magazine editor Ed knew introduced him to a man from Texas who knew a lot about the California reined horse and the difference in the training of the Texas horse and the California horse. After reading the manuscript, Randy Steffen arranged to have HACKAMORE REINSMAN published. Randy was not only instrumental in the book's production, this well-known accomplished artist did the illustrations as well. Ed was always amused at the irony of a Texan being the only one willing to publish a book about the California reined horse.

In 1964, Ed's second book came out, REINSMAN OF THE WEST– BRIDLES AND BITS, VOL. II. It, too, is a best seller. In June of 1977, while conducting a horsemanship clinic in Williams Lake, B.C. Canada, Ed had a fatal heart attack and passed away in the arena. There is a third manuscript waiting to be edited. The epilogue in this book was written by Ed many years ago. In a very real sense, it is his eulogy.

1

How to Tie the Hackamore

1. Place the tasseled-knot end of the 24-30 ft. hair rope (**Mecate**) through the cheeks of the hackamore as shown, with tassel to the front of the horse.

2. Facing the horse, start your wraps in a counter-clockwise direction, making the first turn **over** the tasseled knot.

3. Continue wrapping until there is **one less** wrap than will make the hackamore cheeks tight enough, according to the instructions in the text.

4. Hold the wraps in place with the right hand, then form a loop with the running end of the **Mecate** with the left hand, and pass the loop through the cheeks and **above** the wraps, toward the rear of the horse. This loop forms the reins, so adjust the length of the reins by placing the loop over the horse's head so it rests about six inches back of the withers, and lying somewhat slack from withers to hackamore. (**See Sketches 4, 5 and 6.**)

2

3

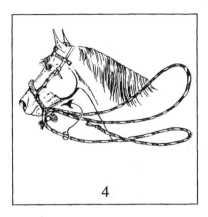

4

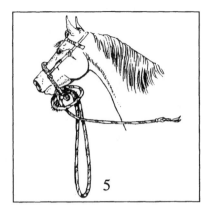

5

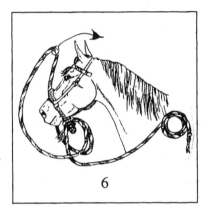

6

7

*Permission to use illustrations from **El Vaquero,** a book by Ernest Morris*

5. Now take one more loose wrap in the same direction as before, with the running end of the hair rope **above** the rein loop, form a loop with this last wrap in your hand, and with the left hand pass the running end down through the loop in your hand to form a tight hitch at the top of the wraps, and just the right distance under the horse's jaw. Now's the time to work all the wraps around tight enough if they've slipped at all during tying. Further adjustment of the reins can also be made at this final stage, if necessary.

6. The running end of the **Mecate** now forms a tie-rope, which can be coiled and tied on the left side of the saddle fork when the horse is being ridden.

HACKAMORE REINSMAN

The fine points of handling the hackamore have been handed down from generation to generation by the early Spanish Californians, who took great pride in their horses. They maintained the art in the business of breaking horses on the American continent. It is fast dying out except in a few places that still keep up the old traditions and system of handling horses.

Today's old timers who learned the business from the early Californians are about all gone, or are too feeble to ride anymore, and young people coming up who are working with horses have not the opportunity to learn first hand from the people who have the knowledge.

If horses were in use today as they were a few years ago, there would be many good horses and many good horsemen, but now the topnotch horsemen are few and far between.

In recent years, due to the influx of people from other states, the methods of handling horses have been changed all over the country. Where a few years ago the hackamore and snaffle bit were used in different states and localities, the grazer bit and new devices have replaced them, and vice versa.

Considering all the fast methods and new equipment used at the present time and comparing the new with the old, the best all-around horses for rein and cow work are still being made with the old time methods. Although it requires extra time and patience on the part of both riders and management the results are worth it.

The secret of making this kind of a finished stock horse lies in the way the reins are handled.

The criterion for this training method is the finished stock horse. This manual is written primarily to help those people who are working with horses every day and who are trying to learn the details of using the hackamore and snaffle bit through actual experience, and who have not had the opportunity to learn first hand.

It is written in successive steps, and in minute detail; consequently there will be many repetitions under each heading to impress upon the reader the value of maintaining a system in handling the reins. The horse learns to work properly by repeating over and over again the same system of handling the reins on his head; the inexperienced horseman also learns by repetition.

11

There are certain basic principles involved in the breaking of good horses that must be followed. After a person knows what they are, it will take some actual experience to learn how to apply them. The most important, and the most commonly known basic principle is doubling, but the others are important too as they all work in conjunction with one another. There is a long step between knowing what the terms of the basic principles are and applying them.

Some horses are naturally light headed, and others are naturally heavy headed, but in the hackamore they all have to be light in order to get the action out of them while they are being worked, and they have to be taught to stop and turn in a certain manner while they are light, or the lightness of the head will do no good. A horse can be ridden with a hackamore, or snaffle bit, but that does not make him a hackamore, or a snaffle bit horse. There are certain requirements in his work when he is ready for the bridle that show whether he is a hackamore or a snaffle bit horse.

In every string of horses there is at least one or more that show up better than the others. These horses are known as **Naturals**.

There are some horses that will work on the rein entirely and never look at a cow, and others that will work on the rein and watch a cow too. Then there are others that have been trained on cattle entirely, but do not know how to work without the cow in front of them. These are known as **Self Workers**.

If given the right training a horse can be a reined horse, and at the same time be a fine cow horse too. Some will always be better than others. The hackamore horse should be given the right kind of work **when** he needs it, and should have steady riding. One cannot ride him once a week and expect to get anywhere with him. The horse should have the right kind of training as he progresses, but should never be soured, or overdone.

The hackamore horse should never be worked when he is good and tired, for he will get heavy and sour on the hackamore. Being worked means stopping and turning. **A hackamore man must have a light hand,** or he cannot get anywhere with the hackamore. The rider can acquire a light hand if he hasn't one already, after he knows the details of handling the reins thoroughly.

This manual deals with the old California style of making stock horses. Riders should always keep an open mind to certain

12

ways of doing things, and to different procedures, thereby not becoming the victims of blind prejudice. Blind prejudice will destroy reasoning power, the powers of observation, and will close the mind.

REQUIREMENTS OF GOOD HACKAMORE AND SNAFFLE BIT HORSES

1. Must have good head position when working. His nose must be down and tucked in, and not up in the air.
2. Must stop on his hind feet with a smooth set, or slide, and must not bounce along on his front feet as he stops. He must stop straight, and not sideways.
3. Must turn on his hind feet with his front feet off the ground, and must be straight from his ears to his tail when turning.
   a. When worked at the set and turn, he must turn on his hind feet, and jump out back the way he came, in one movement after he stops.
   b. When turned completely around, or when he goes into a spin, his front feet must touch the ground every time he is half way around.

FOOT POSITION

When a horse is positioned it means that he knows where to put his feet under him so he can stop and turn properly and easily. When turning with his front feet off the ground and when he sets, or slides, his hind feet have to be under him in a certain position so he can throw himself around and back the way he came, or he will be off balance and cannot do it correctly.

There is **nothing** that can be put on a horse's head that will **force** him to set, or slide, or turn properly, unless he knows where to put his feet. If forced, it will not take him long before he is stopping on all four feet with his head in the air, and turning on his front feet like a bottle.

He cannot be forced by main strength or any contraption on his head and perform easily; his feet have to be positioned before he can do it right and his feet are positioned by the way the reins are handled on his head.

Therefore there are certain basic principles involved in handling his head.

BASIC PRINCIPLES

1. Doubling, or pulling.
Everything done with the horse will go back directly, or indirectly, to the one pull. One pull on the reins, and the horse slides; one touch to the side, and the horse throws himself around and back the way he came.
   a. One pull and slack at the start ends up in one pull and slide at the end.
   b. The light pulls and slacks at the start when turning decreases to one touch and turn at the end.

2. Lightness of head, or light on the hackamore or bit.
The horse has to be light in order to get maximum amount of action out of him while he is being worked. The way the reins are handled on his head is what lightens him up.
   a. Feeling out the horse's head or mouth with the reins, whether it be hackamore, snaffle bit, or bridle. In other words, developing a light hand on the reins.
   b. Slacking the reins between pulls, whether it is light pulls or doubling. Slacking always means a new movement coming up for the horse, and makes him respond to the signal and helps to keep him light on the hackamore, snaffle bit, or bridle.
   c. Working the signal rein with the pull and slack enables the rider to lighten up heavy-headed horses and keep them light, and to keep light-headed horses light.
   d. Set all horses when their front feet are off the ground.
   e. Timing and picking. Time and pick the horse at the end of each movement whether in the hackamore, snaffle bit, or bridle. This is practically the same in meaning as (b) only with timing and picking the reins are slacked, but he is given the signal, or picked at the time the movement is completed, and then slacked and timed and picked again for the next movement. Timing the movements enables the rider to pick the horse for a new movement when he is physically able to perform smoothly.

3.   Ride a balance.
       Riding a balance enables the rider to time the movements
       of his horses by being on a balance with the movements,
       and not against them.

A horse's foot position has a direct bearing on the horse
when he is finished. The finished horse should have a light mouth
and work with his mouth closed on the bit. He can slide, turn, and
spin, and do it easily because he knows how to do it. His nose is
down where it belongs, and he has a light mouth. While the horse
was being hackamored, or snaffle bitted, he was made to ante at the
right time; he was doubled when he needed it; he learned to set
and turn smoothly; his foot position for all working angles became
part of his instinct. In other words he knows how to work when he
goes into the bridle, and if a hackamore horse, **he still has a new
mouth.**
       There is no hard pulling on the reins so all that is left is to
get him bitted up with a tight mouth.
       If he is not positioned when he goes into the bridle, or
does not know how to work, he will be off balance. This will necessi-
tate hard pulling on the reins; something will have to give and it
will be his mouth that gives first, causing him to work with his
mouth open and making him hard-mouthed.
       Each movement the horse makes must be completed before
he can make another, and he should be given time to complete
each movement.
       The slacking between pulls should not be so much that it
would become a jerk on the horse's nose, or mouth, but should be
so that the horse would feel it. Then he will not lose the sensitivity
on the hackamore, snaffle bit, or bridle.
       Many fine horses ready for the bridle are ruined by heavy-
handed riders who do not feel out a horse's nose when working
them. They do not set them when their front feet are off the
ground. They do not slack the reins between pulls, or movements.
They hang on to them after they turn. The horse loses the fine
sensitivity on the reins and does not know what the rider wants of
him. Fine bridle horses are ruined the same way; their mouths
eventually fly open and they end up as mediocre horses.
       It stands to reason that setting a horse when his front feet
are off the ground is correct, and giving a horse time to complete
his movements is correct.

1. Setting with the front feet off the ground.

Take for instance the slide and turn. If the rider pulled up for the slide when his front feet were touching the ground, the horse would have to make an extra hop in order to shoot his hind feet under him, and he would be lunging into the pull on his head, or mouth. If he was set when his front feet were off the ground, he could shoot his hind feet under him in the same movement.

2. Completing the movements.

When the horse comes to the end of his set, or slide, his weight will become evenly distributed again. While he was stopping, whether he was sliding a long way or a short way, depending on the ground, he was more or less on a balance.

Just before the end of the slide there would be slack in the reins, although with a bridle horse the slack would not be perceptible to the eye, but the horse would feel it. Just before his weight shifts to the front feet he should be felt out with the rein and as his front feet touch the ground at the end of the slide he should be picked, or given the signal to turn; then he could use his front feet to throw himself around and back the way he came. The horse has to use his front feet to start his turn correctly, and if given the rein to turn before his slide was completed, he would be thrown off balance.

This shows that giving the horse time to complete his movements is very necessary, not only in breaking horses, but in keeping good horses **good**. The same principle applies to horses that do not slide very far, but have a fast set and turn, only the rider has to handle his reins faster.

These basic principles are used by every good reinsman whether it be hackamore, snaffle bit, or bridle and most of them are used by good grazer bit men.

STARTING COLTS

Starting colts right is very important because the system used throughout starts at the time the colts are started, and is used to gradually improve them until they have learned how to do everything required of them. They go from there into the double reins, and from there to straight up in the bridle. A bad start means a valuable loss of time.

A string should always be started when they are in good flesh, or fat. When they give up there will be no trouble with them, although it may take a cowboy to ride and handle them at the start. If they are started when they are thin and weak, there will be no trouble with them to speak of until they pick up in flesh; then it will always take a cowboy to ride and handle them.

Some outfits start their colts at two and three years old, or long two's. This is especially true in California where the rides are short. They give them the easy rides, and lots of foot work; when the colts are going good they are turned out until the next year.

On the ranches where there is lots of country to cover, colts should be started at from three to five years old. There is lots of difference in starting twos and threes, and threes and fives. The twos and threes start easier and gentle down faster, and is the best age to start them if they are never hurt or overworked.

On the majority of the old time outfits the system of starting colts was to sack them out, after a hind foot was tied up on them and to hobble break them; then saddle them up and climb on. If they bucked it was all right, but it was up to the rider to whip the buck out of them if he could.

It was the old timer's standard policy to whip all colts on the end of the nose when they bucked, and it was done with the sole idea of improving them by making them afraid to buck. When they quit bucking and threw up their heads the whipping stopped. Colts were whipped only while bucking. **(See Figure 1.)**

The real good old time horsebreaker never spurred a green colt while he was bucking, for he believed that spurring would put him on the fight, but he did a thorough job of whipping. He could sit up in a slick fork saddle and pop a horse on the end of his nose every jump with a quirt. It was a disgrace for him to miss his nose and hit him on the head. The only kind of a horse that he spurred was some old chronic bucker which he whipped and spurred at the same time, but he spurred him with the idea of making it tough on him. In those days a rider was not cowboying a bucking horse unless he whipped him.

This was a tough method, both on the riders and horses, because if a colt got by bucking a few times without being whipped he was likely to buck all the rest of his life, no matter how much he was whipped after. Lots of them got to bucking so well after awhile that not many riders could whip them and stay on top. Nevertheless, the old timer knew what he was doing, and he stood for no abuse whatsoever with either cattle or horses.

In those days the horses were not bred up to the fine degree they are today. They were of the mustang variety, or half-breeds from mustang mares and pure-bred stallions. The horses of today are not inclined to buck as were those of yesterday, so whipping as a standard policy is not needed any more. Only in exceptional cases will it do any good. The well-bred horse of today is too high-strung in temperament to be handled roughly.

Figure 1

18

It is better to take more time and work them out on foot properly for four or five days, or a week, before riding them, as this will give them a chance to get over their fear somewhat. If they were ridden right away, they would probably be scared into bucking. After they are worked out on foot for a few days, in all probability none of them would buck when ridden. Especially is this true of the two-year olds past, and threes. If a horse has some age on him he will be more likely to buck.

Every now and then a horse will show up that, no matter what is done to him, if the buck is in him, he will buck some time with the rider; instead of trying to hold him up and keep him from bucking, it is better to let him buck at the start and whip him good every time he insists on it. After he is whipped a few times, he will not be so keen on it anymore. The rider should be in a position to give it to him every time he starts; if he whips him one time and lets him go to the next it is better not to whip him at all. Letting him buck at the start, when he insists on it, gives the rider a chance to figure him out, and he will know what to expect. After the horse is going good, he can do a far better job of bucking, and the rider will not be able to whip it out of him.

If the rider is going to start a string of colts and take them all the way through himself, he should not have over five head, as five will keep him very busy after they wake up and know how to work a little; especially if he hackamores them. If they are feeling too good they will try to take advantage of the rider; they should always be in good flesh and feeling good.

Ride each horse frequently and keep him feeling good for that is when he goes ahead in his work. In other words, get him right and keep him there.

Green colts have to be pulled at the start, but if done right it does not take much pulling even at the beginning. Some have to be pulled more than others. After they are started, it does not take much pulling, only when they need it. The main idea is to have them so they **can** be pulled, or doubled when they do need it. Pulling, or doubling, does not injure the horse physically in any way.

Colts will not learn very much by being ridden straight ahead all the time. There are other things that have to be done with them to put them up where they belong, and keep them there.

In starting well-bred horses, the more time and foot work taken in handling them the easier they will start. They will practically come by themselves to what the rider wants of them. There are times when a rider will have to get a little tough with a colt to keep him in line and make him ante. It only takes one or two stings with a quirt or whip on this kind of a horse when he is being ridden, and he will be doing something. The idea is to have him do what the rider wants him to do to the best of his knowledge and no more. A rider cannot fight this kind of a horse and win, as he will never give up.

Well-bred horses are inclined to switch their tails at the start. They will quit it after they know how to work. Some will maybe switch for two or three months after they are started. This is another reason why they should be started easy. If the rider is inclined to dynamite his colts at the start, the switching will become fixed in their minds. Their tails should not be pulled until they have been ridden for a week or two. Tie them up if they are too long. Well-bred horses are inclined to be cinchy. The majority of them are. They will fall over backwards if cinched too tight when first saddled up. Warm them up first by saddling ahead of time, and leaving the cinch snug until it is time to go, then cinch the saddle just tight enough so it can't be bucked off. There is no need to cut him in two with the cinch.

Too much doubling will quickly make a switch-tail of a horse. After they are started, they should never be pulled unless they need it. They will need it though, sometimes, whether they switch or not. **They should be started without spurs until they are going well.**

In some localities, especially in California, they will be tied up in a barn at night. This gentles them down fast. **They should be tied with a rope around their necks instead of a halter because if they are hackamore horses they should not have anything pulling on their noses except the hackamore.** The halter will serve to make them hard.

The rope should be tied loose enough so that the loop will go over his head. If tight the knot may get over his ears and if he pulls back he can choke to death. A loose horse in the barn is better than a dead one.

A strap buckled around the neck is the best to use first; run the strap through a medium sized ring, and tie the rope into the

20

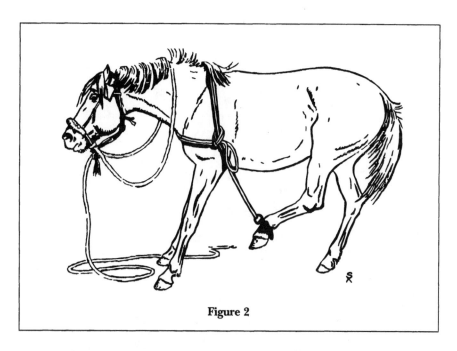

Figure 2

ring. If the ring gets over his ears, and he pulls back, the ring will slip back down the strap, or the strap will break, or tear out.

The first thing to do after a string of colts have been caught up is to tie a hind foot up on them, and sack them out gently and thoroughly. **(See Figure 2.)** Sacking them out is to take an empty sack or piece of blanket, throw it on them gently and easily, being careful not to sting them with it. This takes the fear out of them somewhat. The hind foot should not be tied up too long at one time, or the horse will get tired of standing on one foot, and fight and throw himself unnecessarily. They will all fight the rope at the start.

When the hind foot is tied up, it is better to use a short heavy strap with a D in each end, and long enough to go around the pastern. Then he cannot burn himself with the rope when he fights it.

All colts should be hobble broken at the start. Both the front and hind legs can be hobbled at the same time, although it is not necessary to hobble the hind legs on the majority of colts. After they have been tied up, and sacked out thoroughly it is time to saddle them up and turn them loose with the empty saddle. Some of them buck good and hard, but this does not mean anything at

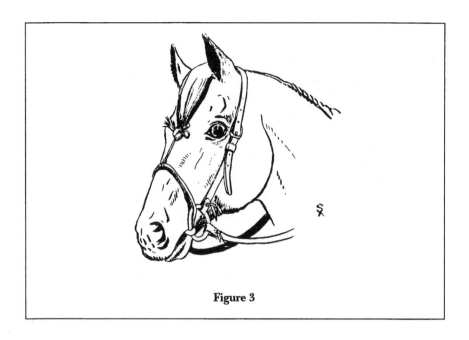

Figure 3

this time. Leave them saddled for three or four hours, then turn them loose until the next day. **It is not good to work too long at one time on green colts.**

The next day saddle them up and turn them loose with the empty saddle for half an hour. They will not buck much this time. Catch them up and put a snaffle bit on them. The snaffle bit should have a fairly long leather string run through the center of the bit, and long enough so that it will come out of each side of his mouth; make a loop over the nose, and tie below his eyes. Then take a light string and tie the loop to his foretop **(See Figure 3.)** This will keep him from getting his tongue over the bit, and it will not be working on the bars of his mouth so much, and he will learn to keep his tongue under the bit. This should be kept on until he is going good.

After the snaffle bit has been adjusted the colts should be checked up. They should not be checked very tight at the start, just tight enough to pull their heads down a little; one rein should be a little tighter than the other. **They should be checked only for two hours at the start.**

If there is no bitting harness to use the reins can be run around the back of the cantle of the saddle and tied there. The horse will begin to give to the bit in a little while. **(See Figure 4.)**

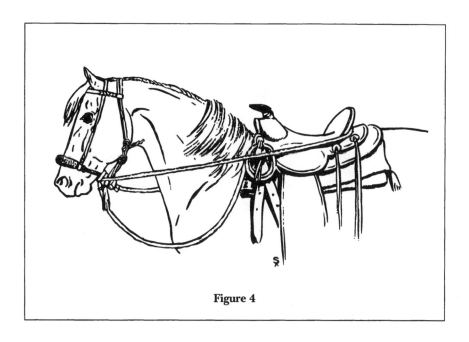

Figure 4

The next day check them a little tighter and change sides on the short rein; leave them checked for three or four hours. After three days of checking with the snaffle bit do the same with the hackamore. A soft hackamore should be used and kept rather loose on the nose while checked. **With either the snaffle bit or hackamore, they should not be checked so tight that they cannot tuck in their noses and get a little slack in the reins.**

DOUBLING OR PULLING

After they have been worked out on foot and checked well, they should be pulled on foot before they are ridden. As they are handled during this working out period on foot, they should be turned around completely on both sides with both the hackamore and snaffle bit. This should be done three or four times a day at intervals.

The rider should walk around with the colt as he turns at first, and then turn on both sides. He should not pull steadily on the rein, but should pull and slack him around completely. When he knows what it is to turn this way, then the rider can pull him around completely, without walking around himself.

The rider can run the rein around the back of the cantle of the saddle on the opposite side to which he is standing, shove the colt's head away from him, and pull and slack the rein, giving him time to turn. A couple of times a day and the horse will soon learn to turn all the way around. Pulling hard should be done with the hackamore, and not with the snaffle bit.

The hackamore should be a soft one, wrapped on the sides with cloth, with a flat piece of leather slipped in between the wraps and the colt's jaws, and tied there to keep from skinning his jaws. The nose band of the hackamore should be where the gristle of his nose enters the bony part of nose, making a slant down to the jaw knot of the hackamore. It should not be too high, or too low. There is more leverage when it is a little low. **(See Figure 5.)**

The hackamore should be rather snug on the jaw, but not cinched down tight. It is not good policy to skin the jaws, although a little skin off will not necessarily spoil them, but they should not be kept sore.

Doubling, or pulling is very important. The main idea is to get them to come around on each side without their sticking, or learning to take their heads away from the rider; they will do this if

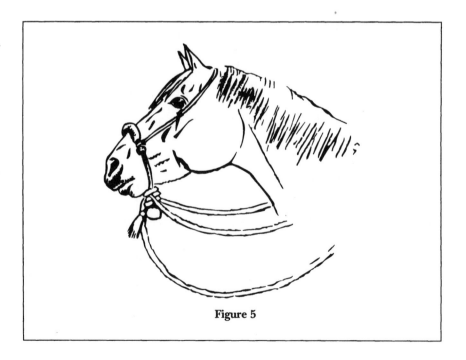

Figure 5

he pulls too hard on them at the wrong time, before they know what it is to turn around with a man on them. The easier it is done the better. They will learn to set their necks against the pull if the rider is not careful how he pulls.

The rider is building them up at this stage so that he can double them without their getting the best of him at any time. They can **learn** to take their heads away quickly.

After the hackamore is adjusted so that it is rather snug on the jaw, and the hackamore reins tied up around his neck so that he can't pull the hackamore off, (a hackamore and fiador is the best to use) tie a fairly long rope into the lead rope of the hackamore, and scare him into running down the side of the corral fence; let him go about thirty feet then take a hip lock, and sit down on him twice on each side, and pull his head away from the fence. Running him down the fence keeps him running straight, and enables the rider to get a better pull on him.

He should be pulled this way two or three times before he is ridden, and he will know what the hard pull is without being able to take his head away.

The best and the easiest way to ride them at the start is to lead them off another horse, providing the rider has some good help. They will never get a chance to run or buck, and they can be pulled this way and that way by the other horse after they have quieted down. This is a very good way to get them limbered up.

Pulling them off another horse will save the rider lots of time and hard work. They should be led twice in the corral and once outside.

If a rider is working alone the best and easiest way to start them is to use the snaffle bit; then double rein them into the hackamore. Some will not need double reining, and others will. They will not be able to take their heads away so easily as there is a lot of leverage to the snaffle bit.

If the rider is working alone and starts all the colts in the hackamore, he has to be careful. He could pull them first off another horse with nobody on them; run him down the side of the fence, and pull his head away from the fence.

When first ridden they should be taken very easy and turned two or three times on each side. The rider should not try to pull too hard, or double the horse until he gets to know more about it. **A half hour is enough until the next day.**

25

The next day the rider should get him galloping around the corral, and try to turn him this way and that way, and when turning, pull his head to the fence as that will make him turn short. Try not to turn him too fast, nor pull too hard, or never run him too close to the fence, or he may try to take his head away and stick there.

The main idea in getting him limbered up is to have him so that when he is going to turn, his head and neck will give a little with the easy pull. If he is pulled too hard at the wrong time and sets his neck, the rider will not be able to pull him around; the horse will then be pulling on the hackamore and may develop into a false double.

A false double is when the horse is pulled hard his neck is stiff, or set, and will not bend. He sets his neck when he knows he is going to be doubled, yet he will stop and turn after a fashion. If he is left like this, he will never lighten up as he should. A horse like this is better off in a snaffle bit until he straightens out.

When he is turned in the corral, he should not be turned completely around as that will confuse him. Turn halfway only. When he turns and faces back the way he came, gallop him back the way he came.

It is important to remember when turning, either hard, or easy, **never to pull steadily on the reins; always pull and slack** 'til he gets turned around facing the way he came, then gallop him back. When pulling hard, give him one big hard pull and slack. As the one pull will probably not turn him half way around, finish turning him with lighter pulls and slacks and gallop him back the way he came.

If he is going too fast the rider will have to give him two, or three, hard pulls and slacks before he gets him stopped and turned back; after he knows more about it, it will take just one hard pull and slack, and he will start shooting his hind feet under him and come around.

Never hang on to the rein after he stops and turns, as he will not be learning to turn if he is hung on to, and he may develop into a limber neck, and try to run away with his head around to the rider's knee.

When pulled hard he should always be pulled on both sides; when turning easily **he should always be able to see the rider's hand as he learns to stop and turn by watching the hand.**

There is always one colt in a string that will not want to turn and will resent it very much; the best way is to ride him first with a snaffle bit. If he does not want to come then, put draw reins on him and he will come then whether he wants to or not. One or two rides with the draw rein should make him give up.

The draw reins are easy to put on and take off; they consist of two long leather reins about eight-feet long with a snap in one end, and a half-inch wide. The snap end is run down through the ring on each side of the bit, and snapped into the cinch ring on both sides.

When a hackamore colt does not want to turn at the start, tie his head to his tail, and let him pull himself around. This will not be teaching him to turn, but will make him give up so the rider can teach him to turn by taking him easy. When his head is tied to his tail, make him turn around a couple of times, then let him stand, or he will get dizzy and fall down with his head under him. **A half hour is long enough for the average colt.**

After the colts get to coming around with the snaffle bit, they can be double reined into the hackamore. Double reining is to put both the hackamore and the snaffle bit on them at the same time. Both reins are used at the same time, and gradually the hackamore reins are used more than the snaffle bit reins, until the colt gets used to turning on the hackamore reins entirely.

Figure 6

27

Remember: in pulling, reach down on one rein, and give him one big hard pull and slack when his front feet are off the ground; always give him slack after the pull; do not hang on to the reins. Turn him back the way he came and always pull on both sides. **Be sure the pulling is not overdone. (See Figure 6.)**

The length of time a colt is ridden in the corral depends on the way he handles. If he comes easy, and can be doubled and controlled, he can be taken out right away.

The rider should be able to handle him as some will want to run, or buck, and when a green colt runs wide open in the hackamore he is out of control. He will have to be pulled too much to get him stopped. **Pull and stop him before he gets to running too fast.**

Sometimes when running too fast or wide open, the colt cannot be pulled; then he is learning to run away, commonly known as stampeding.

Whenever a colt cannot be handled as he should and can get the best of the rider in a pinch, he will find it out very soon. The rider will not make him ante as he should for fear of the horse getting the best of him; then the rider will be stealing a ride on him.

An hour's riding the first time out of the corral is enough, as the colt will be tired and worried. If one is a little snuffy, he could be given a little more.

POINTS TO REMEMBER

1. When turning, hold the hand out to the side where he can see it, as the horse learns to stop and turn by watching the hand.

2. Always use light pulls and slacks.

3. Do not pull any harder than necessary; try to feel out the nose, and mouth, by using the fingers on the reins.

4. When doubling, or pulling, give him one big hard pull and slack on a short rein, and pull when his front feet are off the ground.

5. Do not let him run wide open.

6. Do not hang on to his head as he goes along, or he will get hard on the hackamore.

7. Ride a loose rein at all times.

8. Do not jump him out, or start him quick, as this will keep him stirred up, and the rider will have to hang on to the reins.

9. Keep him as quiet as possible.

GIVING TO THE HACKAMORE

The horse must give to the hackamore at all times in order to learn to work according to the requirements of this kind of training. If he does not give to the hackamore, he might just as well be ridden with a halter.

He gives to the hackamore because he knows that he can be doubled whenever the rider wants to double him.

He has learned to respect the hackamore, and pays attention to it.

He becomes light on the hackamore when he gives to it. When he gives to it, he feels the hackamore when the reins are worked. If he did not feel it, he would not give to it. **(See Figure 7.)**

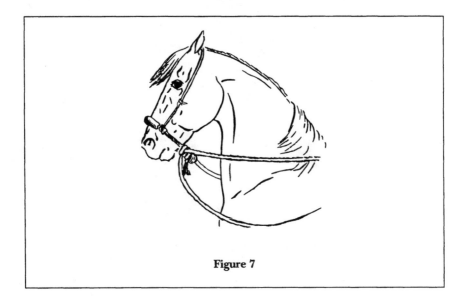

Figure 7

He has to be light on the hackamore before he can learn to slide and turn. When he feels the hackamore he is not being hurt by it.

THE RELATION OF DOUBLING TO THE SLIDE

When he can be doubled easily, he will give to the hackamore, and will throw his hind feet under him a little when the rein is pulled on; also he will tuck in his nose a little with the easy pull. **(See Figure 8.)** When he does this, it is the beginning of the slide.
The rider must feel out his nose, and not pull any harder than his head when handling him.

He learns to stop straight from the start with one pull and slack, **and the rein is pulled straight back to the rider's stomach.**

Figure 8

With this pull and slack the hind feet should go under him a little if he gives to the hackamore. He should be worked with the pull and slack straight back whenever he is set up, and as time goes on he will get better and better at it, and will finally slide.

At the start he should not be running too fast when set up. Many colts have been known to slide a long way in three or four weeks, when the rider has done a good job of starting, and also when the colts have been more or less naturals.

For the average bunch of colts three months is the usual time for them to start to shoot their hind feet under them in good fashion.

Doubling does not injure the horse physically in any way. **It is a means to an end.** Doubling must not be overdone. Through doubling the rider gets the horse up to a certain pitch, then he keeps him there so he can learn to slide and turn.

HEAD POSITION

After the colt is started a most important thing to remember for the next four months is to fix head position. The checking at the start brought his nose down, and he must be handled carefully from now on to keep it down.

The finished bridle horse should work with his nose down and tucked in, and if the colt's nose goes up, it only has to come back down again in the bridle; it is better to take time at the start, and keep his nose down where it belongs. **(See Figure 9.)**

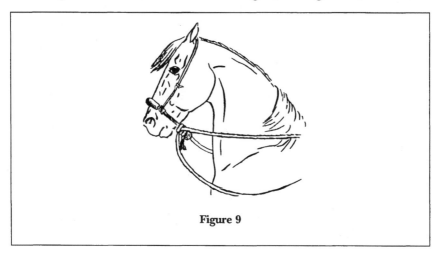

Figure 9

31

If a horse has his whole head up in a rider's face, he cannot work the way he should because he will be out of position.

A horse's natural head position is down, and when his nose goes up in the training process, it is caused by the way the reins are handled on his head.

It should be remembered that a steady pull on the reins, and pulling both reins even will make him throw his nose up as he gets the habit of reaching up with his nose, feeling for the steady pull. This will also make him bob his head up and down.

Tie-downs will keep a horse's head down while they are being used, but will not cure a horse of throwing his nose up as he gets used to the steady pull from a tie-down.

The important thing to teach a horse at the start is to tuck on the hackamore or bit. Tucking enables the rider to keep its nose down through the training process, and a rider can always go back to it later on if the nose starts to go up. **Tucking is used directly and indirectly all the way through the training process.**

TUCKING

It should be remembered that tucking should be used on green colts before they get the habit of throwing up their noses when they are being worked. After their noses are up, tucking will, in the majority of cases, not do much good in fixing head position. **(See Figure 10.)**

On light-headed horses a soft hackamore should be used, and on heavy-headed horses a good stiff hackamore should be used.

The hackamore should be tightened up according to the horse; if he is light, and the rider can feel him out easy on a loose hackamore, or if the horse gives to the hackamore, that is as tight as it should be. If he is heavy, it should be rather snug on his jaw, but not screwed down tight.

Heavy-headed horses have to be pulled more than light-headed horses to lighten them up so they will pay attention to what the rider wants of them. A light-headed horse will not need any pulling at all to speak of.

After the colt has been ridden outside, it is necessary to get him galloping around in the direction the rider wants him to go; always keep him under control and never let him run wide open

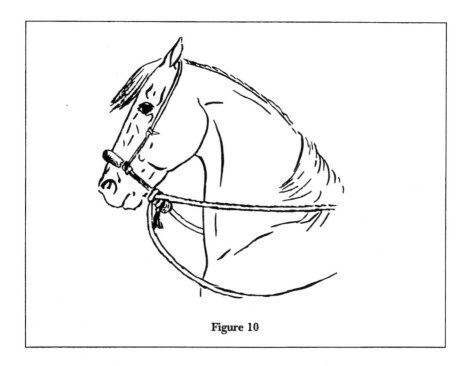

Figure 10

even with the snaffle bit. If he gets going too fast, pull him a little, just enough to slow him down.

Start the colt on the figure eight as soon as possible. This consists of galloping him around in the pattern of a figure eight. Large figure eights should be made at the start, and the rider, when turning, should hold the hand out to the side the colt is being turned on, so the horse can see the hand, and then give him light pulls and slacks until he is going the way the rider wants him to go. If he does not want to turn, pull him hard on each side and go back to figure eighting again.

Figure eighting teaches him to change his leads with his front feet. On the left turn he leads with his left front foot, and on the right turn he leads with his right front foot. Many horses will lead with their left front foot most of the time. Figure eighting makes the colt more nimble and enables him to make very short turns at a gallop and helps to position all of his feet for turning.

When stopping, never pull hard, and never pull both reins even, or the colt's nose will go up; after he gets this habit it is practically impossible to get it back down again by normal means.

As he is walking along, or as he breaks into a trot, take a rein in each hand about even with the fork of the saddle, using the fingers, then give him several light pulls and slacks, with one rein, catch him quick with the other rein and give him several light pulls and slacks, and pull back toward the sides of the rider's hips.

The first pull should be lighter than the second. The rider feels out the colt's nose with a light pull just hard enough to start the nose down and then gives him a little harder pull. This is done on a loose rein, on both sides the same way. **(See Figure 11.)**

This teaches him to bring his nose down with the easy pull. These pulls should not be any harder, or lighter than his head, as he has to feel these pulls. As he starts to give to the hackamore, these tucking pulls will check him and slow him down. He should always be slowed down, or stopped when this is done.

This does not mean that a rider should do this continuously from the time he gets on till he gets off , as that would be doing it too much and would not do the horse any good. Use the legs and feet to urge him into a trot, then tuck him down to a stop or walk.

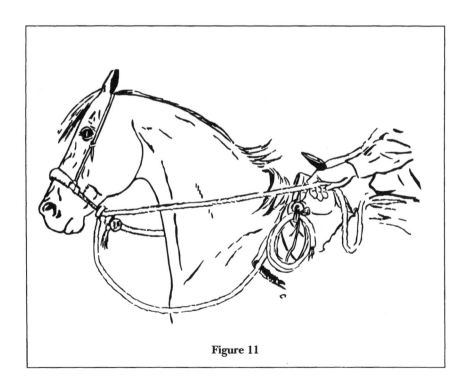

Figure 11

If the horse does not want to stop when this is done, turn him around and make him face the way he came; make him stand for a minute, although it may be necessary to pull him hard to get him stopped.

Tucking is feeling him out with the reins, with the light pulls and slacks just hard enough so he will feel them, but not hard enough to be a jerk on his nose or mouth. It is done also to help lighten him up. Do not try to slide him, or make him stop quick, as it takes quite awhile for a horse to learn to slide, and he has to learn it. The rider has to teach him how to do it, or he will never be able to do it.

From now on till he is ready for the bridle, all the work on the colt will be toward one objective and that is to position his feet so he can slide, turn and spin. Do not try to neck rein, or squaw rein him. Neck reining and squaw reining only cramps the horse's style and action at this time.

After a horse is in the bridle, he has all the rest of his working life to be neck reined in, so there is no hurry about it.

Anybody can get a horse to neck rein around a corner, but that is not a reined horse. **(See Requirements page 13.)**

Some horses learn quickly and others are slow and take more time, especially heavy-headed horses, and they have to be taken very carefully at the start to bring their noses down.

POINTS TO REMEMBER

1. Do not let the colt run wide open.

2. Do not pull too hard when getting him stopped, and never jerk on the reins.

3. Pull back toward the side of the rider's hips with pulls and slacks when making him tuck.

4. Do not try to neck rein or squaw rein.

5. Do not pull both reins evenly.

6. Play with his head, or make him tuck as much as possible **without getting him sour.**

7. Ride a loose rein.

8. Let the horse see the hand when turning.

9. Every horse is different and has to be handled accordingly.

10. Keep him as quiet as possible and do not let him get stirred up.

TEACHING GREEN COLTS TO BACK

Teaching green colts to back is very easy. One of the main points is to not be in a hurry to back them up fifty feet or more. As soon as the colt gives to the hackamore, he will back a step or two, and that is all that is wanted at this time.

If he should back a hundred yards at this stage it would not do him or anybody any good, as he does not know how to work yet and his backing up could not be used.

In actual cow work the horse does not have to back up long distances, but he has to back short distances practically every time he works cattle so there is no hurry in having him back up a long way.

The main point in backing green colts is to not stick them by trying to back them too far at one particular time. If a colt has been stuck, the rider may have a little trouble with him. Back him a step or two at a time and gradually increase it over a fairly long period of time; then the horse can be backed long distances and think nothing of it.

He should be backed a step or two at a time by using either light pulls and slacks with first one rein and then the other, or by pulling both reins even, whichever he gives to the best. **(See Figure 12.)**

The rider should give him several light pulls, wait a few seconds and do it again. When the colt backs a step or two, quit on him till the next day. The rider should make him back a step or two before he quits on him. Stay with him till he backs; after three or four light pulls, pause a little, then try again; the rider should never forget himself and try to make him back by using main strength or jerks after he has stuck.

The rider can always tell when a colt is about to stick and he should quit on him before the colt gets so that he wants to stick.

36

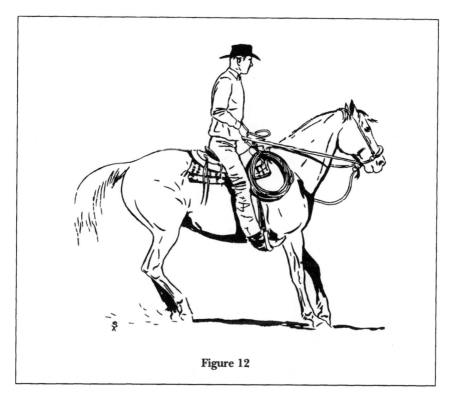

Figure 12

The rider also knows how far he will back and if he does not get in a hurry he will not stick him.

When a colt is stuck backing up, he is sour on it. When starting on it again, it is just like teaching him over again; the rider will have to get him backing a step or two at a time until he has lost his sourness; then he will back as good as he ever did.

If a horse does not want to give to the hackamore, he may not want to back up either, but this is not sticking, as he will back when he has been lightened up.

When the colts give to the hackamore, or bit, they will back a step or two and this is very necessary as the rider will want to back them a step as they are being turned easy from a standstill.

Backing a step as they are being turned makes them throw their hind feet under them in the right position for turning on their hind feet, and they will gradually get the habit of turning on their hind feet. It is not necessary to back them every time they are turned, but enough times so they will gradually get into the habit of coming back on their hind feet to turn.

STUDYING THE NATURAL APTITUDES

There are some colts that are natural sliders and others are not. The natural sliders go ahead faster than the others as their feet are more positioned for what the rider wants of them.

If a rider was in a position to pick out all the natural sliders then all the horses in his string would turn out exceptionally well, but the professional horse-breaker cannot pick his horses; he takes what is given to him and does the best he can with them under the circumstances.

After a string of colts has been ridden for three or four weeks, all the best actioned colts can be picked out very easily. Even before they have been ridden, the best actioned colts can be picked out with some study.

Take, for instance, a bunch of colts that are ready to start and are running loose in the corral; by watching their movements carefully and the way they handle themselves with their hind feet, the smooth actioned colts can be picked out. **(See Figure 13.)**

Practically all well-bred horses have good action, but there are some when playing and running loose, that will use their front feet a good deal when stopping. These are known as prop-setters,

Figure 13

and require careful handling so they acquire a smooth set and turn without bouncing along on their front feet to a stop. This kind of horse should be trained with the fast set and turn.

Every now and then colts will show up that will stay juggy (lazy, lethargic, lacking in energy, thick-headed) for several months, although they will have lots of life and action when they are not being ridden. They will be behind in their work. They will always wake up after awhile, and when they do, they will generally go ahead fast. Sometimes they will take to bucking.

Their dispositions will have a lot to do with their progress. Some may be inclined to be mean and kick and strike for quite awhile; others may want to buck, although the age at which they are started will influence this trait a good deal. Some will be gentle and kind, and others sullen, etc.

To the professional horse-breaker the dispositions of the colts are a side issue as he knows that they all have different personalities and gets around them accordingly.

If all the horses have good action and life the rider is supposed to bring out the action and life in them when they are being worked and he puts on the form to the way they work. (**See Requirements on page 13.**) The rider brings out the action and life in the horse when he works him, but he cannot put the action and life into the horse when he hasn't got it. If the horse hasn't good action and life, he will never make much of a horse.

LIGHTENING THE COLTS ON THE HACKAMORE

It should be remembered that colts have to become light on the hackamore in order for a rider to get the maximum amount of action out of them while being worked.

They get light on the hackamore when they give to it, and they give to it through the use of doubling, and the use of one rein with the pull and slack, as the pull and slack gets to mean a new movement coming up for them and makes them respond to the signal.

Tucking also helps to lighten them up besides keeping their noses down until they find out what it is all about. From the time the rider takes them out of the corral and has them so he can double them, to the time they can be made to go where he wants them to go, is the lightening up period.

The heavy-headed horses have to be lightened up, and the light-headed horses have to be kept light.

In handling at this stage the rider is using mostly the light pulls and slacks with first the one rein and then the other to keep the colt tucking in his nose, and letting him see the hand when turning him with light pulls and slacks.

From now on the rider should be able to use one hand as well as the other and have the same system of handling the reins with each hand; he will have to do this until the horse's training is finished.

While the colt is in the hackamore, and even into the double rein, the rider should always use the hand on the side that he is turning on; this means that he must keep changing hands on the reins as he works his horses. This is done because the horse started out by watching the rider's hand, and he learned to stop and turn because of it, and if the rider does not change hands on the reins, the horse will go out of position.

When he stays out of position, he will get one-sided; he will come up too high off the ground with his front feet when he is turned; he gets so that he will lug on the hackamore and get hard. He will also fall short on the half turn.

After he gets to know how to work, keep him working in the style or form in which he learned to work; the quickest way to get him to go out of position is to neck rein him too quick and continuously.

The hackamore horse should be judged by the form in which he works and not by the way he neck reins.

When a horse gets to know how to work up to the time he goes into double reins, one rein is worked a little shorter than the other, and the rider keeps changing hands on the reins, whichever side he is turning on.

When the horse is set up, one rein on the side he is turning on is a little shorter than the other, then the horse knows what side he is coming back on; working the one rein shorter than the other would not be perceptible to the eye, but the horse would feel it.

As he is double-reined and as he learns to carry the bit, when he is ready to be worked a little on the bridle reins he gradually learns to stop at all times with the reins pulled even, and turns at all times by neck reining.

There are always exceptions to the rule though. Now and then some will show up that can be neck reined continuously from the time they are first started right through till they are finished and do not go out of position.

These are few and far between. Some of them may be very light, and others not so light, and then others are very heavy on the hackamore. The ones that are very light should have a soft hackamore on them so they will not throw up their noses, and it should be loose, but not so loose that the rider could not double them if he had to.

The very light colts will not need much tucking as their noses will come down anyway. These colts are light already, so they will not need lightening up; that is what the rider wants, so the idea is to keep them light. **It should be remembered the harder the hackamore is pulled on, the harder the horse gets on the hackamore.**

This is where the light pulls and slacks that are no heavier than his head are used to keep him light and keep his nose down.

On this kind of a horse a rider can develop a light hand by always feeling out the horse's nose before working him, and as he works him. Feeling out the nose is always done with a touch and slack.

The ones that are not so light should have a heavy, soft hackamore on them tight enough so that they will feel it. The rider should tuck them to a stop now and then and turn them easy, always using one rein.

The use of one rein and being doubled when they need it will lighten them up in a few days. They should be pulled if they do not want to give to the hackamore; but if they are improving slowly, do not pull them; working one rein with the pull and slack will get to mean a new movement coming up for them, and they will lighten up.

The rider should not double them unless they need it, and should double on both sides when he does, so they will not get one-sided. **Always make sure the horse needs it before doubling.**

When a colt does not want to give to the hackamore, or pay attention to it, and wants his own way more or less, he should be doubled; but the rider should give him the benefit of the doubt before pulling, and not double him for every little thing he does that is not right.

41

At this stage the horse should be moving when pulled, or he will most likely rear up because his feet will probably be in the wrong place. **(See Figure 14.)**

If he starts to rear let his head go back and jump him out; as he gets going, pull him hard when his front feet are off the ground; then he can get his feet under him so he can come around.

The hackamore should be on them so they feel it at all times, but not screwed down tight as their noses will get numb after awhile, and then they will not be able to feel it.

Heavy-headed horses should have a large stiff hackamore on them at the start, rather snug on their jaw, but not cinched down tight; they have to be doubled more than the others to loosen

Figure 14

them up; they will generally stick their noses out when turning, therefore, it is better to pull them once or twice a day for two or three days. A thong can be put in their mouths and tied up over the wraps of the hackamore. This will lighten them up quicker. Leave it on them for two or three days.

Run them down the obstacle or fence or barn and pull them on the side the obstacle is on to make them stop and turn short; then run them back on the other side and pull them into the obstacle. Pull with one big hard pull and slack when their front feet are off the ground. **(See Figure 15.)** Although it will not hurt them, or injure them in any way, it must not be overdone. After they learn to give to the hackamore, they will need very little doubling. The

Figure 15

light-headed horse gives to the hackamore from the start, and the heavy-headed horse does not.

If, when they are tucked with one rein on either side, their hind feet start to go under them a few inches, then **the rider must not over do it.**

If the horse is ridden for two or three hours, move the hackamore up or down on his nose every hour so he will keep feeling it.

When he begins to lighten up, put a medium-sized soft hackamore on him, as he will try to get away from the stiffness of the hackamore and throw up his nose.

Heavy-headed horses need steady riding. A colt that is naturally lazy will need waking up once in awhile. He will take advantage of the rider by going to sleep and will not lighten up as he should. Wake him up and make him stay that way, but he should not be stirred up so much that he will want to be dancing and prancing all the time.

All the colts will learn more with two hours riding a day than they will with long rides, and they should be ridden every day if possible. After they are going well, they will need longer rides.

Remember that if a hackamore is kept screwed down tight on the jaw all the time, the soreness of their noses will cease to bother them after awhile, and they will really get hard on the hackamore.

The rider should use good judgment and not over-do any one thing, especially doubling; colts have to be pulled at the right time, and it will not hurt them; **but when they are doing all right leave them alone,** then the rider can always double them when he has to.

A tired colt should never be pulled unless he gets so rank there is nothing else to do. When tired, he will get heavy on the hackamore; the rider should work the colt as easy and slowly as possible; then he will not have to pull him.

A tired colt can learn to do a lot of bad things in just a few minutes if he is pulled too much in the hackamore. One of the worst things he can learn to do is to lunge into the pull on his head without turning and with his head around to the side.

There are many riders that double their colts too much, because they don't understand the basic principles of handling the reins and the different steps that follow one another. Understanding the basic principles and the application of the different steps when it is time to apply them eliminates unnecessary doubling.

The rider should circle the colts as much as possible, with or without cattle; circling helps to position their feet and teaches them to run on a loose rein.

Remember: do not get in a hurry to get them finished. Do not crowd them. **Nobody can break a good horse in a hurry and anybody can spoil him.**

Some may need shoeing right away and they should be shod on the hind feet at once. They should be shod all around if they are sore on the front feet too.

Letting a colt get sore on the front feet to make him slide is a matter of personal opinion. However, a horse that has been shod all around at the start will slide just as far as one that hasn't.

There is a tendency with the snaffle bit to ride the reins; the rider should watch this and handle the snaffle bit the same as the hackamore with light pulls and slacks and not hang on to the horse's head.

The rider is creating with the colts the system by which they are going to learn to work the way the rider wants them to work. There is a definite system and definite steps to be followed in hackamoring colts in order to bring out the action and life in them.

FORM, CLASS, AND JUDGMENT

The main objective from now on is to get them coming the right way so the form can be put to their work. **It is a slow and easy process.** The form in which they work makes the class when they are ready for the bridle.

They stop in one movement with their noses down, and tucked in; they turn with their front feet off the ground. They can be jumped out at any angle the rider wants to make. They stop straight and turn with their body straight. They turn halfway or spin, and they do it easily. They work smoothly. **(See Figure 16.)**

A rider must use good judgment at all times and understand the use of the principles; they are not hard to learn, or study out; they come easy with practice. He must not deviate from them by getting in a hurry, as there is no short cut for training this kind of a horse.

Knowing the basic principles forward, backward, and upside down will do no good if the rider does not use good judgment. Each horse must be handled according to his temperament. There are times to leave them alone and let them work. There are times to handle them very easily, and times to get rough with them. There is only one way for a rider to get to know when to do these things and that is by figuring out each horse and by experience in handling horses.

It is better to be a little slow than to be too fast, because if the rider crowds them he will sour them every time.

Any horse can learn just so fast and if he is crowded too much he cannot hold or retain what he has learned before; he gets confused, and all of a sudden he cannot seem to remember anything. He is bound to get sour and will most likely spoil.

Figure 16

STARTING ON THE SET AND TURN

The set and turn is very important in breaking horses, as the set and turn takes care of all the working angles of the well-reined stock horse. Everything done with the horse through the training process is designed to build up the set and turn so that the horse can do it smoothly and easily when he is ready for the bridle. It also gives form to the way they work.

As the colts progress and lighten up and can be galloped around where the rider wants them to go, they can be started on the set and turn. It takes quite awhile for horses to learn to set and turn well, and it takes from eight to twelve months (on the average) before they are ready for the bridle.

The first thing to do is to find a suitable place to work them at the set and turn. A good place is in a square corral, or along a board fence, or barn. Turning them into the fence or barn makes them stop and turn short. **It is a good idea not to work them around the barn in which they are kept, as they will want to get back to the barn and this will take their minds off what the rider is trying to teach them.**

Before working them at the set and turn, warm them up a little. Circling for a little while is a good workout for them.

Then take a colt and gallop him down the fence, or barn, at an easy stride. After he has gone fifty, or sixty feet, more or less, take one rein, and when his front feet are off the ground, give him a little pull straight back to the rider's stomach. At the same time say "whoa" so that he will learn to associate "whoa" with stopping after awhile; it will help him to learn to stop.

If he has been lightened up, he will feel this little pull and his hind feet will go under him a little. The rider should slack the rein right away, as he feels the colt's feet go under him a little with the easy pull. **(See Figure 17.)**

The colt should not be pulled hard enough to make him throw his nose in the air. The rider can feel him out as he pulls and can tell how hard to give him without making him throw his nose up, and at the same time making him throw his hind feet under him a little.

He will not slide or stop quickly, but his momentum will be checked somewhat; after the slack from the pull, let him go four or five steps before the reins are worked again, then get him stopped

47

Figure 17

as quickly as possible. Tuck him down to a stop.

He may go twenty or thirty feet past the pull, but that is all right. The pull should be on the side the fence or barn is on, and he should be turned on the same side.

If he does not want to give to the hackamore, or feel it, double him on both sides on a gallop to loosen him up.

When teaching the set and turn, **always make the colt stop before he is turned.** Make him wait a few seconds; then turn him. This is known as making him **dwell** and teaches him to wait for the rein before he turns. After awhile he will come to know that he has to stop before he turns and will shorten his stop by himself.

THE DWELL

The dwell is important when teaching colts to set and turn; it is a pause between movements with a slack rein either after a stop, or turn. This pause is longer than the ordinary slack or pause between pulls when the horse is being worked fast. The horse is made to wait for the rein or the next signal. It might be a few seconds or a few minutes. He is made to dwell after he stops, and before the reins are worked again to turn him back. After the pull to stop, the rider lets him go four or five steps before the reins are worked again. This interval between the first pull and the time the reins are worked again becomes the dwell after he begins to stop in one movement. **(See Figure 18.)**

The set and turn are always worked together.

After the colt has stopped, turn him back the way he came, using light pulls and slacks and hold the hand out to the side where he can see it. As he gets two thirds of the way back, give him a little scare so he will learn to jump out after awhile.

Figure 18

49

When turning, and this is important, try to take the angle with the hand out to the side that will bring him back on his hind feet as he turns; then gallop him back the way he came and do the same on the other side. **Always turn on the single rein. (See Figure 19.)**

It is not good to have him too close to the fence or barn or obstacle when turning him. If he is too close, move him out a little and give him room to turn, for if he is too close he might stick there and learn to rear up, or bull on the hackamore or bit.

When doubling, get him on a gallop, but not really fast; reach down on one rein about a foot from the fork of the saddle, and as he is galloping away, give him one big hard pull when his front feet are off the ground; then slack the rein. If he is not checked sufficiently, give him another pull and slack; when he has

Figure 19

stopped enough so he can turn, finish turning him easily, and make him gallop back the way he came. Then double him on the other side.

Doubling at the right time makes him pay attention. **Too much doubling is worse than none at all,** as he may take his head away from the rider on both sides and run away with him; he may fight the hackamore by striking at it, or he may dog it and refuse to pay attention to anything.

About three times on each side is enough at the start for the set and turn. **If it is overdone, the horse will sour on it.** After the horse is sour all the work on him that far is spoiled, and it will take time to get him back where he was. While he is that way he cannot be worked at it until he forgets it somewhat; he should be taken very easy when started on it again.

The pulls and slacks will become lighter as the horse learns to turn. After the horse is turning pretty well half way, the rider should not try to spin him or turn him completely around. He has to be ready for the complete turn, or he will go out of position.

The horse should be worked at the set and turn for a few days, then given a rest on it.

The rider should always figure out his colts so he will not overdo them. **What he can do with one he maybe cannot do with another. The rider has to use good judgment at all times.** A horse is not mentally capable of absorbing much at one time, so in working him remember there is another day coming.

SUMMARY

1. Do not let the colt run wide open.

2. Work him against an obstacle so he will learn to stop and turn short.

3. Warm him up a little before setting and turning.

4. After fifty or sixty feet hold one rein and when his front feet are off the ground, give him a light pull, say "whoa", slack the rein as his hind feet go under him a little. Pull back to the rider's stomach.

5. Do not pull hard enough to make him throw his nose up.

6. He will not slide, or stop quick at first.

7. Let him go four or five steps before the reins are worked again; get him stopped easily. If he goes twenty or thirty feet past the pull that is all right.

8. If he doesn't feel the pull, double him once on both sides.

9. Do not double him while he is standing still.

10. Doubling at the right time makes him pay attention.

11. Do not double unless it is necessary.

12. Make him stop before he is turned so he will wait for the rein.

13. Use light pulls and slacks when turning, and let him see the hand when turning.

14. Take the angle with the hand that will bring him back on his hind feet as he turns. As he backs a step, turn him easily while backing.

15. Do not keep him stirred up.

16. Just before he gets faced back the way he came, give a little scare so he will learn to jump out after awhile.

17. Do not turn too close to the obstacle.

18. Do not try to spin or turn him completely around.

19. Do not try to hold him to it with the reins, or he will get to lugging on the hackamore.

If colts are being worked on cattle all the time, the rider will not have to keep such a close watch on them to see that they get the right kind of work as he would have to do if they were not working cattle. They should have the easy end of the riding when working cattle, and they should not be worked too fast or too long, especially when they are getting tired.

In the course of a day's ride, the rider can find a good place to work them at the set and turn a few times, such as the bottom of a gulch where it is somewhat level and smooth and with a bank to work them against.

They must be worked at the set and turn without cattle, too, and they must always be worked the same way with the reins. They should be circled whether they are working cattle or not, as this keeps them running on a loose rein.

SNAFFLE BIT, SET AND TURN

With the snaffle bit the method is practically the same as the hackamore. With the snaffle, the rider has to be more careful with head position. The colt's mouths can harden up quickly as the bit is sliding across the mouth all the time. Hanging on to the reins will toughen their mouths quickly. They should not be worked at the set and turn if they do not tuck on the bit well. When teaching them to set, if they do not want to give to the easy pull, take their heads a little to one side.

If the rider takes their heads to one side with the hackamore, he will be teaching them to take their heads away from him. With the snaffle bit this does not make any difference.

The chin strap should be adjusted so that when the horse is pulled, the rings on the bit will not chew up the corners of his mouth, and the headstall should be fairly tight.

EVERY DAY WORK

When working cattle the rider should not try to work his horses **too fast,** and should **not let them run wide open after an animal.**

If the rider jumps the horse out and lets him run wide open, he would find himself hanging on to the horse's head with the reins, which will make the horse hard on the hackamore. It would also spoil him for running on a loose rein which he learned to do when he was circled.

After the horses are going well, the rider knows how fast he can jump them without stirring them up; as they get better, they can be worked faster.

If the rider is rather close to an animal when he heads him and the colt has to make quick stops, **the rider should never forget himself and pull hard and steady on the reins** as doing that a couple of times will ruin the head position for good.

When the rider pulls hard he is going back to main strength and is forgetting the basic principles. **The same system of handling the reins must be maintained all the way through.**

He should take one rein and pull and slack and pull and slack with the rein out to the side a little, so the colt can see the hand.

A horse can see the hand when it is out from the leg a little and a trifle below the rider's hips.

If the horse is not going to slow down, the rider should reach down on one rein and double him with one big hard pull and slack; this one pull should pretty nearly stop him if he knows what it is to be doubled properly; then finish turning him easily with lighter pulls and slacks.

If the rider has to double the colt over two or three times, he should not do it anymore at that time, but should circle him to bring him back. If the colt is too fast for a bunch of slow cattle, the rider should not hold him back with a steady pull on the reins, as that will make him bob his head up and down.

Bobbing the head up and down becomes a habit very quickly; but the horse will get over it, after he has been ridden on a loose rein for awhile with light pulls and slacks. He gets the habit of feeling for the steady pull on the reins.

A colt that is too fast for a bunch of slow cattle is very exasperating to ride and should not be behind cattle until he has slowed down more.

Circling will slow him down better than anything else for he will soon find out that he is not going any place, and will learn to run on a loose rein.

Because a horse has lots of life in him, is nothing against the horse, and a horse with lots of life can be just as quiet as a dead head, and when he is finished he will be a better horse than the dead head. It is up to the rider to see that this excess life is not misplaced.

The rider should work his colts on an animal in the open, and should continue to do this as much as possible. He should get in behind a yearling, a two year old, or a good strong cow, and follow it until it slows down; then get in behind it after it has had a breathing spell; the animal will not run fast this time and the rider should turn and circle it on both sides for awhile. **(See Figure 20).**

Then get another animal, as the first one will have had enough for that time, and do the same thing while the colt is fresh.

Get him up close to the animal when turning in a circle, and circle the animal on both sides; make the animal turn in small circles. **(See Figure 21.)**

He is learning to follow the animal and at the same time learning to crowd it.

This should be remembered: When crowding an animal around in small circles, the horse's shoulder should be at the animal's shoulder, or neck. Should the animal fall down the horse will then be able to jump clear of the animal without falling himself. If the animal is being crowded in back of the shoulders and happens to fall, the horse will likely trip and fall over the animal and perhaps injure the rider.

The rider can always tell when the horse is watching the animal. His ears will be working back and forth and he may try to bite it when crowding.

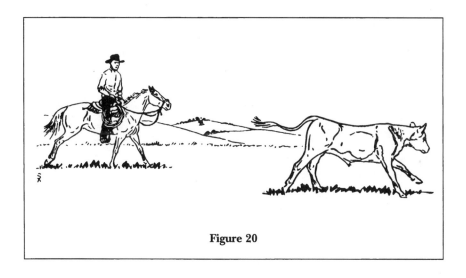

Figure 20

Figure 21

Always work him on an animal when he is fresh. Do not overdo it. **Two animals at any one time is enough.** Make sure the horse does not get sour on it.

As the colts progress from day to day **they should not be worked on cattle every time they are ridden.** They should be worked at the set and turn without cattle in between times.

They should be worked at the set and turn by themselves about four times on each side, **the rider always being careful that he does not sour them on it.**

When working them either on cattle or by themselves, try to maintain head position. With both the hackamore and the snaffle bit, head position is maintained by tucking.

When setting the colts with either one of them the long rein is worked just enough to bring their noses down and that is all. Working the rein this way also tends to keep them stopping straight.

If a colt wants to throw his nose up when stopping on one rein, catch him quick with the other rein, just enough to bring his nose down and that is all. Turn him with light pulls and slacks with the hand out to the side and on an angle that will bring him back on his hind feet.

Letting him go four or five steps (after the pull before the reins are worked again) is done so the colt will be looking after awhile for a new signal between the slack after the pull and the time the reins are worked again, and he will shorten his stop by himself.

These four or five steps after the pull becomes the dwell after he begins to stop in one movement.

After he begins to stop in one movement, the length of time the rider gives him to dwell in becomes less all the time. The rider automatically judges this himself.

After the first pull and slack, do not keep catching him with other pulls and slacks in order to get him stopped quick, as that will make him bounce and spoil his slide.

Working him against a fence or barn teaches him to turn on his hind feet and teaches him to shorten his stop and stop straight.

Do not work him at the set and turn too much over long periods of steady riding, or on each separate ride, as their hocks and feet will get sore, causing them to favor their hind legs and spoiling their work. Especially is this true when the ground is hard and dry.

A rider should never try to make the horses do things just right on any particular ride at this stage before he quits on them. If he does, he will sour them every time. He should just go along as easily as possible with them and at the same time make them ante at the right time.

GUIDE IN KEEPING HEAD POSITION

The rider must not make any of the following mistakes when teaching the colts to stop, or set, or they will throw their noses up in the air: (See Figure 22.)
1. Pulling too hard on the reins.
2. Not slacking the rein quick enough after the pull.
3. Not pulling when their front feet are off the ground; catch them in the air when pulling to set.

Figure 22

The two most common causes of making them throw their noses up is pulling too hard on the reins and not slacking quick enough after the pull. In other words, trying to slide them or trying to make them stop quicker.

SNAFFLE BIT

With the snaffle, the rider should always feel out the mouth as he works the horse and not strong-arm him; if the colt is strong-armed, his mouth will get tough caused from calluses formed on the bars of his mouth.

It is useless to try to maintain head position with the snaffle bit if the rides are too long. If the rider has to make a long circle on a colt and then get in and help work cattle on him when he is good and tired, the rider will not be able to do fine work on him.

Under these conditions it would be better to use running rings, although the rider will not need them all the time.

It is important to remember that running rings should be put on before the colt has learned to throw his nose up, or they will not do any good. **When the nose first starts to go up, they should be put on.**

The long running rings should be used; these consist of an inch strap slit down the middle to within several inches of the end and a snap in the end that isn't split; this end snaps into a ring on the cinch between his front legs and the two split ends have adjustable rings in them. This kind of ring gives the horse more freedom of head (sometimes called **Running Martingale.**)

INDIVIDUAL CHARACTERISTICS

As the rider knows, each horse in his string has a different personality and temperament, and he has each colt figured out. He knows automatically how each colt will react to certain things and he knows that what he can do with one in a certain manner he cannot do with another, although they may be full brothers. He will have to go about the other differently to get the same results.

For instance, one can be worked a long time at one particular thing before he sours, and another will sour in half that time.

The way the horses handle themselves at this time with either the hackamore or snaffle bit, will be different. Some will be limber-necked and others not.

The limber-necked colts will bend their heads and necks way around to the side as they are being turned, but they are all turned on the one rein principle with the hand out to the side where they can see it, and the correct angle to the hand that will bring them back on their hind feet as they turn, always using the light pulls and slacks. **(See Figure 23.)**

The rider should not try to hold them to it, or straight with the reins because after their turn has been speeded up they will not bend their heads around to the side anymore.

Some will be inclined to be a little stiff when being worked; when they turn they will not bend their heads and necks around at all, but will turn with their bodies perfectly straight, although they will be very light on the hackamore and come around easily and quickly and can be doubled very easily. **(See Figure 24).**

These colts do not give to the hackamore correctly. When a horse is giving to the hackamore correctly his nose will come out to the side a little with the easy pull, or his neck may bend a little right behind the ears when his nose tucks in and comes out to the side. His hind feet will also go under him a little when he is being taught to set.

All of them are handled with the one rein basic principle at this stage no matter how they do things, as this principle will teach them to turn on their hind feet with their front feet off the ground.

Some of them may be natural sliders and others natural prop-setters. The natural slider gives the rider lots of time to handle his reins when he works him, and the prop-setter does not. Care must be taken when teaching them all to set by catching them just right while they are in the air so they will not bounce. They must all give to the hackamore, or feel it; especially the prop-setter.

Figure 23

They will all slide if the proper care is taken in handling the reins.

Practically all hackamore horses, although there are exceptions, will get hard on the hackamore in time and that is why they must be started in the double reins as soon as they know how to work.

If a good hackamore horse has become hard there is nothing that can be done to him that will lighten him up again such as doubling, or jamming around, or scaring, because he knows how to work. Maybe he is getting tired of paying strict attention to the hackamore all the time. It may be a form of sourness.

If a horse has not been started in the bridle, ride him with a hair hackamore, one half mane and one half tail. He will lighten up with this in several days; after he is light again, put him back in the regular hackamore.

Figure 24

When he gets hard in the double reins use the hair bosal until he lightens up; then put him back in the regular bosal again. Do not leave it on him, or it will have no effect on him after awhile, and will make him hard on it, and it may also make him switch.

The bosal is used when bridling the horse, or in double reins. It is made exactly as the hackamore only smaller in size, so as to fit in between the sides of the horse's nose and the bent out tops of the bit. In size it is about three eighths of an inch in diameter or smaller so as to not chafe the sides of the horse's face. Anything over this size is a hackamore according to common usage. Technically they may be the same. Quien Sabe?

After a horse lightens up well, it is better to put a lighter hackamore on him as a heavy hackamore will make him hard on it.

A rider should have all the different kinds and sizes of hackamores he will need at the time he needs them, especially if he is in the business of training horses.

All rawhide hackamores should be shaped to the horse's nose and jaw before they are used. Then, with usage they will pull down to an exact size and stay that way. A stiff hackamore is one that has a rawhide core in it. A cable cored hackamore cannot be shaped correctly either at the start or with usage.

A soft hackamore is one that has no core in it. They are made with just the braided strings, and the degree of stiffness depends on how tight the strings are braided.

One starting hackamore is all that is needed.

Starting hackamore, rawhide cored, 7/8ths or 3/4ths inches in diameter.

A light stiff hackamore 5/8ths of an inch in diameter.

A light stiff hackamore 1/2 inch in diameter.

A rather heavy soft hackamore 3/4ths of an inch in diameter, or a trifle smaller.

A light soft hackamore 5/8ths of an inch in diameter.

A light soft hackamore 1/2 inch in diameter.

A stiff double rein bosal 3/8ths of an inch in diameter.

A soft double rein bosal 3/8ths of an inch in diameter.

A hair hackamore 5/8ths of an inch in diameter.

A hair double rein bosal 3/8ths of an inch in diameter.

The soft hackamores should be used on naturally light-headed horses.

THE RELATION OF DOUBLING TO THE TURN

Doubling is one big hard pull and slack to turn the horse when he has to be doubled whether he is standing, walking, moving slow, galloping, or running fast. **(See Figure 25.)**

The horse learns to slide and turn through the use of doubling. One light pull on the rein and the horse slides; one light pull to the side on a single rein and he turns halfway with his front feet off the ground.

This is where turning him against an obstacle so he will have to turn short and pulling on the single rein makes him come around with his front feet off the ground.

Figure 25

There needs to be just one pull and slack against the obstacle with the rider hurrying him up a little as he turns, and he will turn correctly. The main point is to **not hang on the rein after he starts to turn.**

Hanging on to the reins eliminates the one touch and turn. After the horse knows how to turn, he will not have to be worked against an obstacle any longer, only when he gets so that he does not want to do it correctly.

PULLING ON THE TURN

It was stated at the start that the rider should not double a green colt when he was standing still or moving slowly, but now that the colt knows what it is to be doubled and come around, he will not be so likely to rear when pulled.

The reason colts rear is because their hind feet are in the wrong place to come around and that is all they are able to do when pulled hard.

Many a colt is slow to find his foot position and if a rider catches him unaware he will rear when pulled. When this happens he should be moved quickly, and as he gets going, pulled, so that he can find his foot position and come around.

Rearing becomes a habit very quickly, and should be avoided at all times. If the colt has learned to rear sometime when the rider gets him in a pinch, he will take to rearing again.

At this stage, a colt can be pulled when he is moving slowly, walking, or standing. When a colt needs pulling, he should always be warned first before he is pulled hard.

Give him a light pull to get him started; when he starts to come, pull him hard with one hard pull and slack, and let his head go back straight again, and as he straightens, and as his front feet touch the ground, pull him hard again and again until he makes one complete turn anyway, or not over three half turns. After each pull, slack the rein completely before pulling again, and do not hang on to the rein. Let his head go back straight between pulls. **(See Figure 26.)**

If possible he should be pulled this way against an obstacle.

His front feet will be coming off the ground as he comes around. The rider is feeling out the horse's head when he pulls, and pulling so that the front feet will come off the ground as the horse comes around, and he is not pulling so that it is a series of hard yanks without giving the horse a chance to come with each pull.

The hard yanks would be just fighting the horse without giving him a chance to come with each pull. The rein should not be snapped on his jaw too hard as he is pulled, although there must be slack in the rein after each pull.

Give him a chance to come with each pull.

Too much pulling this way makes his nose fly up. Pulling this way with the snaffle bit is done the same as the hackamore.

Figure 26

THIS SHOULD BE KEPT IN MIND

Pulling this way helps to position the colt's feet for turning. When the colt is running, pull with the one pull and slack, then finish turning easily. This makes him shoot his hind feet under him so he will learn to slide.

SPEEDING UP THE TURN

A horse is ready to have his turn speeded up when he turns on his hind feet slowly. Taking the angle with the hand out to the side has brought him back on his hind feet, and he turns properly slowly with one or two light pulls and slacks.

The light pulls and slacks have decreased to one, or several; now that he turns on his hind feet, it is time to speed him up. Although some will be doing it very well they should be speeded up with the rest of them just the same, so that if sometime they go out of position or get confused, they will remember how to turn.

If they are well-bred, high-strung horses, they should be taken very easy. A rider can scare more life into a horse than he **can by whipping him.** One little sting on this kind of horse goes a long way. If a rider can find something that will make some noise without stinging too much it will be better to use than a quirt, or whip.

The rider should get him along a board fence, or barn, or a bank of some kind to turn him against. Have whatever he is going to hit him with in the opposite hand to the side he is going to turn on.

If he is going to turn on the left side the rider should have the quirt, or whip in his right hand; have him close enough to the obstacle so that he will have to turn short.

Start to turn him easy, and as he is half way back hit him on the shoulder, release the rein altogether, and as he straightens out facing back the way he came, hit him a lick over the rump. If using a quirt, be careful not to hit him too hard. **(See Figure 27.)**

He will be surprised and get out of there in a hurry. Get him slowed down and stopped easy. If he is a high-strung horse, do not scare him too badly.

If this has scared, or stirred him up badly, let him get good and quiet again before giving it to him on the other side. When he

Figure 27

is quiet do the same thing on the other side. Quiet him down again by going on a slow ride with him for an hour or so, **then unsaddle him for that day.**

With horses that are not so high-lifed, it is easier to do this. The rider should keep his horses as quiet as possible.

The next time he is ridden the rider should get him up against the obstacle again and give him a little pull, and as he starts to turn give him a little scare with the movement of the rider's body and he will throw himself around and jump out fast with one light touch on the rein.

After this the rider should not be turning the colt fast all the time as he will get tired of doing it and get sour on it. **He should always help his horse to turn with the movement of his body.**

If the colt does not have to be worked fast on the turn, avoid turning him fast just because he will; then he can always be turned fast when the rider wants him to.

When turned fast at this time, the rider should always let him jump out a few steps before he stops him, or before he has to turn him again if he possibly can.

Speeding up has straightened out the limber-necked horses a good deal, but their necks will bend a little yet and this is as it should be as they will not work perfectly straight until they are further along.

Speeding up the turn fixes it in their minds so they will remember it. If this is not done, after awhile the horse will get it in his head sometime that he does not have to turn.

The horse must turn when the rider wants him to and not when the horse wants to.

Always touch and slack the reins and no heavier or lighter than the lightness of the horse's head.

POSITIONING THE FEET BY CIRCLING

From now on the turn can be shortened up when the horse is being circled. Shortening his turn means to start circling at a fairly large circle, say 50 feet in diameter and gradually narrow it down to a small circle. After several complete circles in one direction gallop him in the opposite direction without stopping, and narrow it down again.

At the start he learned to change his leads with his front feet, but as the circle narrows down he will be a little awkward yet when changed . As the circle narrows down, galloping him in a small circle helps very much to position his hind feet for turning.

It will not take very many times of figure eighting him in a small circle before he gets good at changing his leads with his front feet, but it will take quite awhile at circling before he can make very small circles at a gallop. He should not be forced at any one time to do it, as he will not be able to follow his head around until he knows where to put his hind feet.

He is turned as he has been on one rein with the hand out to the side where he can see it, by using light pulls and slacks, and with the right angle to the hand to make him turn to the degree of turn the rider wants to make.

As the horse is galloped in a small circle, the rider can tell by the way he is galloping whether he is having any trouble in making the turns; if he is doing all right, every now and then, bring him in closer, or very short for a couple of leads, then let him back out in a larger circle again.

As he gallops in a narrow circle, the rider can help him to keep galloping with the movement of his body. On a gallop the rider's body goes back and forth with the movement of the horse.

When galloping in a small circle, if he is having any trouble making the turns, he will want to break into a trot, and the rider can help keep him galloping by moving his body back and forth with the movement of the horse.

It will take a fairly long period of time to get him down to a real small 4 to 6 foot circle, and when he is able to do it, the rider can shorten him up to the half turn, and wind him up in a spin. **(See Figure 28.)**

When the rider is working the horse he is working the reins with the pull and slack, and after he gets down to a small circle, the rider must time him with each pull and slack; when his front feet are about ready to touch the ground, the rider should be feeling him out and as his front feet touch the ground pull and slack him in closer.

Figure 28

When the rider first begins to bring the horses from the very small circle to the half turn, he should be careful and not try to crowd them into doing something they are not able to do at this time.

The horse can do the half turn, and then he will be in a position to make one complete turn. If he does it nicely, he could be turned once again, although on the third half turn, he may not make a good one, but he will come around with his front feet off the ground.

After the last half turn always jump him out and start circling the other way without stopping. **Do the same on the other side, or he will get one-sided.**

It may take quite awhile to get his feet positioned for doing this and in the meantime he will be worked at other things.

THE SPIN

The spin is a repetition of the half turn. The horse has to use his front feet to start his turn every time he is half way around. His hind feet have to be in the right position, or he cannot do it. The horse is balancing himself on his hind feet as he spins, and his hind feet have to be far enough under him so as to be on a balance.

If the horse knows how to turn half way properly with a light pull and slack, he can turn all the way around with another light pull and slack and he will. The idea is to give him some practice at it. The horse should never be worked at it until he gets sour, or he will want to fight the rider on it for a long time.

Turn half way against the obstacle; as he starts to jump, catch him with the single rein with the hand out to the side, feeling him out, and as his front feet touch the ground give him another pull to turn again. These pulls to turn are no heavier than his head. Take the angle with the hand that will bring him back on his hind feet while turning.

There will be no obstacle for him to turn against on the second half turn, and the rider should give him another light pull as his front feet touch the ground. It may take several light pulls and slacks to make the second half turn with the rider hurrying him up a little, and keeping him turning on his hind feet. When he completes the second half turn, he will be up against the obstacle that he started on.

70

Then on the third, or last half turn he should really be hurried up, and as he straightens out, he should be given a little tap over the rump with something that will scare him into jumping out.

Always make him jump out on the last half turn, then he will not go out of position and boil in one spot.

When working the horse this way, **do not over-do it,** as he has to find out what it is all about; work him at it now and then, and he will do it right if given enough time. If this is over done, he will bend his head and neck around to the side a little before he turns. This will make him fall short on his turn. **The rider should quit on him before he starts to do this.**

Whenever he is doing nicely, and suddenly goes back in his work, the rider should never blame the horse; he should place the blame on himself, as he has overdone him. He should think back and try to find out just how it was done, then try to avoid doing it again.

The horses at this stage have set and turned and they know more or less what is wanted of them. They will not slide far, or stop quick, but they should be doing it pretty well.

Every now and then the rider should run the horse into a corner of the corral, or any place where there is an obstacle, and set them up. Just before he gets into the corner and before he starts to stop himself, give him a good pull straight back when his front feet are off the ground, but not hard enough to double him, and not hard enough to take his head to one side. **(See Figure 29).**

Figure 29

71

The purpose of this is to make him throw his hind feet up under him, and also to find out that he can put his hind feet up under him. This will help him to learn to slide.

If he is run too much straight into a fence or barn, after awhile he will get to dodging to either side and this will take his mind off what the rider is trying to teach.

WORKING AN ANIMAL

The rider should work his horses on an animal all he can without souring them. He should work them on **soft or smooth** ground so there is nothing to catch their feet when they start sliding.

After they get so they are no longer scared of an animal and will get in close and follow and crowd the animal, the rider should not do it anymore, as they will not want to pass the animal when the rider works them at the set and turn.

They will be watching an animal by this time. When the horse passes the animal he will be in a hurry to get back to it. **When he goes past the animal a little, the animal will turn toward the horse instead of away from him, then the horse has to set and turn to get back to the animal again.**

When he passes the animal, the rider should work him on one rein with light pulls and slacks, with the rein held low down and out to the side a little by the rider's leg; the horse can see the hand there.

If he wants to go too far without stopping or slowing down, the rider can haul him around on one rein with heavier pulls and slacks. The pulls may have to be heavy ones to get him turned around so he can go after the animal again. **(See Figure 30.)**

Do not double unless it is necessary, or unless he refuses to pay attention; doubling will take his mind off what the rider is trying to teach him.

The reins have to be handled with the same system, or basic principles at all times, and the rider should not forget this and use any old way to stop him.

The rider should not use the other rein at all while doing this, even if the horse's nose goes up a little while getting him turned around after the animal **and he should always pull according to the lightness of the horse's head.**

The horse will be watching and pretty soon he will begin to stop short to come back to the animal; when he does this, to make short stops, catch him quick with the other rein pulling behind the short rein to bring his nose down and no more. **(See Figure 31.)**

Slack the rein after his feet go under him, then turn on the single rein with the hand out to the side as he turns. He is doing this mostly by himself with a little help from the reins and because he likes to play this way.

Catching him with the other rein as he stops to bring his nose down is the same as tucking, and it keeps the horse stopping straight as he is supposed to stop.

When he stops in one movement and turns in one movement, it is time when another very important basic principle of handling the reins comes in. This is timing and picking.

Now he is stopping in one movement, which is what the rider is building up to when he sets and turns the horse by himself, and the rider is slacking the reins after the pull so that the horse will learn to stop in one movement.

Figure 30

Figure 31

TIMING AND PICKING WITH CATTLE

When the horse goes past the animal's head, pull one rein on the side he is turning on; then catch him quick with the other rein just enough to bring his nose down.

As the rider feels the horse's feet go under him, he slacks the rein on the side he is turning on. The other rein is already slacked when his nose came down.

As the horse sets, or slides, the rein is slacked just before the stop is completed; the rider must time him while he is doing this. As the horse's feet go under him, the rider slacks the rein, and just as the horse's weight is ready to shift to the front feet, the rider feels him out with the rein. As his front feet touch the ground, the rider picks him to turn with a light pull and slack out to the side. He then goes after the animal again and passes him on the other side the same way. (See Figure 32.)

If the horse runs choppily, the rider will have to handle his reins very fast, **but he must maintain the system because the horse learns by repetition.**

74

Figure 32

On horses that handle themselves smoothly, the rider will have lots of time to handle his reins, and to feel them out as he works them.

When the horse is picked, the rider is timing his movements and feeling out his nose a little so he can pick him at the right time, after he has slacked the reins between pulls.

Picking is never a jerk on the horse's nose, or mouth; if his nose or mouth were not felt out as he was picked, it would become a hard unnecessary jerk.

Feeling out the nose or mouth has to be done lightly and fast; otherwise it would become a steady pull on the nose. Then the horse cannot feel the signal when it is given to him, and he cannot be timed correctly; he will also get hard on the hackamore.

When a rider is on a balance, timing becomes a natural instinct with practice. Feeling out the nose helps the rider to time his horses, and timing them enables him to pick them at the right time.

When a horse is having a little trouble with his foot position, when setting and turning with an animal, after he stops, and when trying to come back, he may come up off the ground a little with his front feet once or twice before he throws himself around and back the way he came.

The rider should not let this become a habit. After the horse does this several times and fails to come around at the end of his slide, he should be picked with a hard pull at the right time so he will know that he has to turn and come back at the end of his slide.

When working an animal this way, lots of times the animal will run in back of the horse, and will be on the other side of the horse after it has been headed off; then the rider will get a chance to turn his horse around with a complete turn.

When the rider picks the horse for the half turn after the stop, he slacks the rein, and as his front feet touch the ground, he picks the horse again for another half turn and goes after the animal again. The horse then has made a complete turn and has done it correctly. This is a very good way to help position his feet for the spin.

After the horse gets to be good at this, the rider should take care not to sour him.

When the horse begins to stop in one movement, the rein that he is being turned on is always pulled straight back to the rider's stomach, and the other rein is worked just enough to bring his nose down. With the snaffle bit, if the rider is using running rings, they should be taken off as they will hamper his turn. Use draw reins to keep his nose down.

SLIDING AND TURNING WITHOUT THE COW

Colts are started out with the one pull and slack to set and turn, and they are worked that way all through the training process and end up that way by sliding.

When they are first started on the set and turn, they give to the hackamore, and when the rein is pulled straight back, their hind feet will go under them a little. As time goes on they will get better and slide a few inches. They improve as they go along, and get so they stop quicker and quicker, and slide a little farther all the time. They finally end up sliding a long way. There is always a dwell before they are turned which is never entirely eliminated.

The sliding horse must always be handled so that he always gives to the hackamore. Some naturally give to the hackamore, and some are not so quick to give; others are very hard to get loosened up so they will give to it. When they give, they feel the reins when they are worked; if they did not feel the reins, their hind feet would not go under them.

Regardless of how they are, it is the rider's business to make them all give to the hackamore, for he makes their hind feet go under them by the way he handles the reins. **All horses with good action, regardless of breeding, will work on their hind feet if the rider knows his business.**

The sliding horse should always be worked on good sliding ground. There is always a dwell in the reins before they are turned. The dwelling horse is the sliding horse. **When the horse is sliding, there is the same light pressure on the reins all the sliding distance, until it is time to slack the reins at the end of the slide.** The dwell gives the horse a chance to slide farther and farther. **(See Figure 33.)**

Figure 33

The rider must not crowd him when he is doing all right. If he is set up once or twice in a day, and he does it well, **let him alone.** He must work true at all times. **When setting and turning with an animal, the rider does not let him dwell.** He is picked when his stop is completed.

THE FAST SET AND TURN WITHOUT THE COW

The difference between handling the sliding horse, and the one with the fast set and turn is that **there is no more dwell in the reins with the fast set and turn after he begins to stop in one movement.** There is just the slack in the reins between movements with no steady pressure on the reins. This set and turn is fast and it is also smooth.

It is harder on a horse than the slide, as he is putting forth a lot of action and energy in a short space of time.

He will also slide some distance, but not so far as a good sliding horse. He has to slide somewhat; otherwise he could not do it smoothly. He learns to dig in with his hind feet instead of sliding far, and he uses his front feet to throw himself around and back the way he came. **(See Figure 34.)**

He stops and starts his turn in the same motion. If he is going very fast he may have to prop, or brake himself with his front feet before he has stopped enough so that he can turn, **but it will be smooth.**

A good sliding horse can have a fast set and turn too, **but it will not be so fast as the set and turn horse.** Stopping and turning a horse with cattle is a fast set and turn. The majority of well-reined horses that have been trained on cattle have the fast set and turn.

In order to learn the fast set and turn the horse has to learn to be picked at the right time. **The rider has to time his movements correctly and pick him at the right time.**

When he begins to stop in one movement is the time when he is picked for the turn. When he begins to stop in one movement, his hind feet have to go under him, or he cannot do it. He will slide a few inches.

This is where the fast set and turn comes in. When the rider pulls the horse to set, he slacks the rein as he feels the horse's hind feet go under him; **then as the front feet are about ready to touch the ground, he picks the horse for the turn back on one rein out to the side.**

78

The rider has to time his movements and handle the reins with the movements of his horse.

The rider handled the reins the same way when he worked him at the set and turn with an animal.

After a horse gets good at this, he never slides any farther than he has to. He uses his front feet to start his turn and to throw himself around and back the way he came. This set and turn is very catty and takes effort on the part of the horse.

He should be on an easy gallop and not running too fast when he is worked this way. **The rider should be careful not to over do it.**

When a horse is worked at the set and turn this way he should not be set straight without turning until he gets good at it. If set straight, he will try to turn to either side.

After he is ready for it he can set straight, **but the dwell must be put back in the reins, or he will start bouncing.**

The rider should remember to watch head position at all times by remembering what makes the horse throw his nose up. **(See Guide to Head Position Page 57.)**

Figure 34

FALLING SHORT ON THE TURN,
OR GOING OUT OF POSITION

When the turn was speeded up, throwing himself around and jumping out in the half turn became fixed in the horse's mind, and he now does it with one light pull and slack out to the side.

As he goes along he may begin to fall short on his half turn or go out of position because he is forgetting where to put his feet. **(See Figure 35.)** He also may be getting a little lazy or getting a little sour.

When this happens, the rider should give the horse several light pulls and slacks and hurry him up against an obstacle; then he will come back to it again.

If he is sour on it the horse should be left alone for awhile till he forgets somewhat. Then he should be again worked against the obstacle to make him do it right.

Figure 35

All horses will sometimes go out of position, but this is nothing to worry about as they will come back to it again. The rider may have to work them a few times as he did when they were not so far along to get them back in position again.

Get him up against the obstacle and hurry him up even if he has to be stung with a quirt once or twice; the horse knows how to do it and he is supposed to work when the rider wants him to work and not when the horse wants to. **The rider should use good judgment and not fight him on it.**

DRAW REINS

When using draw reins, the rider should snap them into the cinch rings on each side. **(See Figure 36.)**

Figure 36

The running slack in the reins makes it a strong arm rig as it is very hard to feel out the mouth with them on. **They should be used only for short intervals.**

Draw reins are good for certain things at certain times. They are especially good for certain kinds of spoiled horses and horses that do not know how to work, but have been ridden for a long time.

The reins should not be pulled even and should be worked with the pull and slack at all times, because they toughen a horse's mouth very quickly and make him throw his head up against a downward pull of the draw rein. They should be used when working the horse then change back to straight reins again.

If used right, draw reins help to position a horse's feet for turning by backing him a step or two as he is being turned, and holding the hand on the side he is being turned on out to the side quite a ways so he can see it and holding him to it with the other rein.

The rein he is turning on is worked with the pull and slack, and the other rein is pulling and slacking too, but holding him to it. They are also good for forcing a horse to stop although he cannot do it correctly with the draw reins on him.

There are some horses that do not want to shoot their hind feet under them when learning to set, and on these horses the draw rein will enable the rider to time and pick his horse so that he will be able to stop and come back. The horse cannot slide with the draw rein until he has learned to set his neck against the downward pull of the draw rein, and by that time his nose will be up. On horses that already have their nose up, it does not matter about head position. The draw rein will make them work if handled right.

The horse is handled the same way as in the fast set and turn.

Work him against an obstacle, and when stopping take his head to one side a little with the pull and slack; catch him quick with the other rein after the first pull; then catch him again on the next bounce with another pull and slack until he is about stopped. Then time and pick him for the turn. Do not make him dwell before turning.

As he is stopped between each pull and slack, he will come off the ground with his front feet a little, and just as he is about stopped and as his front feet start to come up, pick him on the single rein to come back. **Make him jump out and back the way he came.**

Wake him up when doing this, and while stopping him this way hold out the hand and rein on the side he is turning on so he can see it. Work the other rein with the pull and slack to hold him to it.

A horse like this is not a green colt; he is used to almost everything, but does not know how to work and is asleep most of the time.

After being worked six or eight different times this way, he will know that he has to come when he sees the hand out to the side and feels the pull. Then the draw reins can be taken off and straight reins used.

When working him with straight reins, the rider should use a squaw rein as it would be easier to handle.

The squaw rein will keep him working as the draw rein did as he feels the other rein, which will keep him working straight as he can at this time.

When he starts to shoot his hind feet under him a little, the rider should put him in a hackamore and work him so that he completes his movements, putting the dwell in the reins. **He should be made to give to the hackamore.**

Draw reins are not needed on green colts except for pulling at the start, but as they get to working it will not do them any harm to ride them with the draw reins once in awhile.

For a colt that has gone out of position draw reins are very good if handled easily. Backing the colt a step or two with the draw reins, and turning him at the same time makes him throw his hind feet under him in the proper position. He only needs to be worked this way for a few times on each ride; several rides should fix him up.

All hackamore colts should be ridden with the snaffle bit now and then, so the rider can go right to work on them if he has to put a snaffle bit on any of them.

Draw reins are good for forcing a horse into certain positions and for doubling most kinds of spoiled horses.

LASSOING OR ROPING

Green colts should have a rope swung on them in the first two weeks of riding. **It is better to get them used to everything at the start.**

No matter if a colt is exceptionally touchy or not, the rider should get him used to the rope in the beginning, as he will give up faster at that time.

There are many horses that have been ridden a long time and still are very dangerous to rope on. In fact they are far worse than a green colt. As soon as the rope leaves the rider's hand, they will shy and spin, winding the rider up in the rope; after the first spin the rider is practically helpless.

This comes from not getting them used to the rope at the start. Many riders put off swinging a rope on a horse that is inclined to be a little brave, and when they do, the horse is worse then than he would have been at the start. When he does try to catch off him, nine times out of ten the horse will be looking for trouble.

A touchy colt should have the rope swung on him in the corral. It should be a small corral so the horse can't get to running too fast, and if he is exceptionally touchy he can be hobbled, and then the rope can be swung on him, care being taken not to scare him unnecessarily. **The rider should stay with him till he gets used to the rope in the corral.** This might take several days.

After the colt is used to the rope in the corral, then the rider can swing it on him in the open. This should be done over a period of a few days **not all in one day.**

The horse should become used to having the rope swung and thrown all around him and dragged behind him, before catching anything off of him.

At this stage the best way to catch off him is first in the corral because he does not know how to stop and turn. Outside he would get to running too fast and then he would be out of control.

If possible the rider should not catch on him in the open until the colt knows how to follow and crowd an animal, and then it is easy to catch on him. **A light animal should be used at the start so the colt can hold it easily.**

The main point at this stage is to not get him scared into running too fast until he has found out what it is all about.

When the colt knows how to follow, the rider should take in behind the animal and not swing his rope to catch until the animal has slowed down.

Then the rider will have a chance to handle his horse and rope and catch the animal too, and the horse will not learn to run as if he wanted to run away. **(See Figure 37.)**

Figure 37

When running the animal to catch it, the colt should be handled on a loose rein the same way as when he wasn't going to be roped on. That is why the rider should not swing his rope to catch until the animal has slowed down. **He should always run on a loose rein.**

If he swung his rope at the start the horse would run too fast and would not feel the pull on the rein. Then the rider would have to double him to get him stopped.

Many riders handle their reins nicely when they are not roping, but as soon as they start to rope they will take up all the slack in the reins; the colt loses the feel on the reins and gets hard on the hackamore. **This should be avoided. The harder the hackamore is pulled on, the harder the horse gets on the hackamore.**

After the rider catches two or three animals in the open the horse will find out what is wanted of him, but after the animal is caught the colt will not stop quickly because he does not know how to stop yet. **Most of the roping should be done in the corral at this stage and on medium weight calves which he can hold easily.**

The rider should catch the calf in the corral then get off and tie his rope hard and fast to the horn of the saddle by using one-half hitch; this half hitch goes under the rope that holds the calf at the horn and then up over the horn and over the dallies. **(See Figure 38.)**

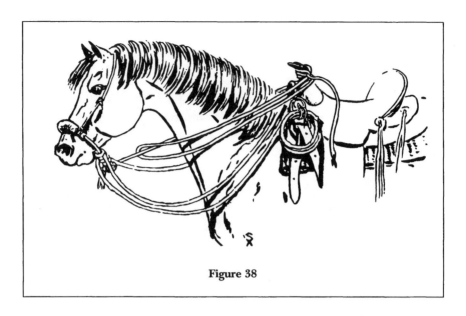

Figure 38

The loose end of the rope goes under the neck on the opposite side from the rope that holds the calf and is tied there. It can be tied or run under the other rope and brought up to the saddle horn again and tied there. The horse will then be tied on both sides and whichever way the animal goes, the colt will be pulled around that way. The rope should be tied this way just snug so it will not pinch the colt's neck as the animal pulls him around.

With this type of training the horse always faces the rope.

After the rider catches, he should be careful how he handles the reins. He should not pull both reins even and not pull steady on them, or the horse will get to boring into the hackamore and will not feel the pull. **Stop with one rein.**

The rider could hard tie, then he would have both hands free to use in getting the horse stopped if he wanted to. He should be careful not to get the horse tangled up in the rope.

Get him stopped so he can see what he is doing. He will not slide or stop quickly at this time.

When the rider is on the ground, he should stay at the colt's head and make him hold as the animal pulls him around. **Two or three calves are enough at the start.** The colt will learn more little by little.

Give him plenty of time at the start. **If he never learns anything bad, there will be nothing bad for him to forget.**

Figure 39

BACKING ON THE ROPE

When a colt gets an idea of what it is all about, more or less, he can be started backing on the rope a little. The rider should not try to make him run backwards, for he will back no farther on the rope than he knows how far to back without the rope. If he gives to the hackamore, he will back three, or four steps, and he will back no farther on the rope.

When the rider is catching calves off the colt, when backing on the rope, especially when catching the hind feet, he should get the colt up as close to the hind feet as possible as the kicking animal will scare him back. This will keep him from sticking. **(See Figure 39.)**

Five or six calves is enough at the start. **Do not rope on him too long at one time at this stage.** If he sticks he will remember it a long time. When he sticks he is sour on it. **He should not hold an animal very long at the start, or he will want to come up on the rope.**

Catch a post on him now and then and back him up. The dallies would not have to be tightened down very tight, and the rope will sometimes scare him into backing farther than he ordinarily would back. Care must be taken in backing a colt so as to never get him sour on it.

The fast step off is very seldom used with this style of training because it will ruin head position, and make a colt hard on the hackamore. After the horse gets to sliding, he will slide after the catch when the rein is pulled on.

It is not a good idea to catch calves on green colts in the open as the colt will have to run fast to catch the calf and then they will be out of control. The corral is the best place at the start.

A colt should always be tied up for a long time when holding a calf by himself because if he gets scared, he could turn around and run away with the calf, choking it to death. The horse should not be started too quickly after the calf, or he will get excited after awhile and get to lunging into the hackamore. **(Note: Horse was drawn without rider for clarity's sake. Never turn horse loose with calf tied in this position.)**

USING JUDGMENT

When a string of horses is this far along and is able to set and turn with an animal, and setting and turning without the animal fairly well, it should be remembered that **they did not get this way in a few days or weeks.**

In about three months their hind feet should be starting to go under them nicely and they should be turning half way properly. **Just because they are doing all right is no reason that a rider should try to work them as fast and as long as a bridle horse.**

They should be worked as fast as they are able to, or know how to work, **and no faster,** and worked so that they do things properly to the best of the rider's ability on that particular ride.

The way they have been handled up to this point has been to build them up so when the rider pulls them up for a set their hind feet will automatically go under them a little every time. **(See Figure 40.)**

When they do this the rider has got them coming the right way. It is now just a matter of giving them time with no crowding, and they will get there.

If a horse will shoot his hind feet under him a little every time he is set up, it does not mean that he can be run out and stopped and turned as well as a bridle horse, although he may do it as well on an animal a few times.

The rider is still building him up so that his work will be true at all times when he is ready for the bridle. He is always feeling

88

Figure 40

out the nose or mouth and not trying to see how far he can slide the horse because if he does, he will find out that he will be pulling too hard on the reins and not slacking quick enough, causing him to bounce, and making him throw his nose up.

The rider is always timing his horse in handling the reins; when he slides a little the reins are slacked so there's no extra pull after he has slid as far as he can. **He should always be turned after the set.**

Turning him after each set does not mean that a rider has to turn him fast, or jump him out each time, but should turn him a little, or quarter ways anyway and turn slowly. If the rider has to turn fast he can always do so if he does not sour the horse by doing it too much.

The rider should not be setting him up all the time. It is all right to do this once in awhile, but if done too much, the horse will get so that he does not want to run out, and will try to stop before the rein is pulled on, or not want to run out, and will try to stop on his front feet.

If he is set up too much, especially after he knows how, he will get so that he will plant his front feet, coming down stiffly and hard and will not want to come back smoothly. The rider will not be able to pick him to come back. If the horse gets this way, it will take a long time for him to get over it.

The rider should be careful where he sets his horses, and particularly not on rough ground unless it is absolutely necessary. This is especially true in a sagebrush country, and in the summer time when the ground is hard and dry, as the horses' feet will stick, making their hocks sore; also the hind feet will get hot.

The best time to get a string of horses sliding is when the ground is wet. Another thing that will help him to learn to slide is setting while going down hill when the ground is wet. If the ground is hard and dry and has a smooth hard surface and a little down hill it is a good place to set him up on. A smooth surface where the ground is level is a fine place too. The rider knows the temperament of each horse in his string and he can begin to work faster as they are ready for it.

If the horse wants to work too fast, the rider should get him slowed down again by taking him easy and making him wait for the rein.

It should be remembered that when they are sliding pretty well, and when moving at a fast clip, they will not be able to stop completely with one pull and slack, although they will slide quite a ways.

After they slide as far as they can with one pull and slack, let them go a few feet before pulling again. When pulled again, they will slide to a stop.

If pulled on again right after the first pull without putting a dwell in the reins they will learn to bounce and bore into the hackamore.

METHODS OF HANDLING THE REINS

When the horse begins to work an animal well, the rider must have a system of handling the reins; he must be able to handle the reins without confusing the horse or throwing him out of position as he times him.

As the horse gets so that he can stop short and come back to the animal, the rider must be able to handle the reins fast, keeping always to the basic principles of handling the reins.

NO. 1 METHOD

One fast method of handling the reins is to hold both reins even in one hand at the saddle horn with no slack in them; then give both reins eight inches of slack and hold the reins even again at that place, in one hand.

As the horse stops short to come back to the animal, the rider should hold both reins in one hand with the eight inches of slack in them. He pulls one rein on the side he is turning on several inches below the other hand that holds both reins.

He pulls one rein when the horse is in the air, and he pulls back toward his stomach. The horse's nose will come out to the side a little as the rider pulls him, then the other rein catches him at the same time and brings his nose down. This is the same as tucking. The slack in the reins after each pull straightens his head each time.

After the set he is turned on the single rein with the hand out to the side. The hand holding both reins must be slacked so there will be no extra pull on the other rein.

As the animal is being worked, the rider changes hands on the reins at the place where both reins are held even and uses the hand on the side he is turning on.

This is a very fast method to use. A rider can work the reins as fast as a horse is physically able to perform. It is too fast at the start, but is fine to work after the horse gets so he can stop short and come back in one movement.

The reins are always worked with the touch and slack.

NO. 2 METHOD, OR SQUAW REIN

Holding both reins in one hand as the horse is being worked, with one rein longer than the other, is another method of handling the reins. This is commonly called squaw reining. This is a very good way to fix head position. At this stage, the horse should not be worked fast with this method as it has a tendency to stick him at turning. The rider has to be careful to see that the reins are not pulling even when he first begins to work this method.

The main points of the squaw rein is to help fix head position, and also to keep the horse turning with his body straight as he is supposed to turn. For turning easily and slowly, squaw reining brings the nose down and fixes head position.

A wide squaw rein should be used. When turning, make sure the reins are not pulling even. As he turns, the rider's hand comes in toward his body a little so there is slack in the long rein. That is why a wide squaw rein should be used.

The use of a wide squaw rein enables the rider to bring the hand toward his body so as to turn on the single rein and the horse can see the hand too.

A rider should never try to throw the horse around with a steady pull on both reins. If he does the horse will get to lugging on the hackamore and get hard quickly; the rider will then be going back to main strength and will be pulling too hard.

The reins are worked with the touch and slack at all times. When the horse is turning fast, the rider gives him several light pulls and slacks. The first one is to get him started; then, the rider as he starts to turn, hurries him up with the movement of his body. The reins are always worked so that the horse comes back on his hind feet as he turns. If he knows that he is going to turn, it will take just one pull and slack for him to turn right. Giving him several pulls and slacks enables him to get in the proper position to turn on his hind feet and the rider will then be giving him a chance to come back on his hind feet.

When being turned slowly with the touch and slack the horse will bring his nose out to the side a little. The other rein then catches him and brings his nose down, at the same time keeping his body straight as he turns. However, he will not be perfectly straight at this time.

If the squaw rein is used when circling, the rider should see that both reins are not pulling even, or the horse will not circle properly. When the rider pulls and slacks the rein, he should bring the hand toward his body as he does it, so as to give slack in the long rein.

When the squaw rein is used the horse gets to know that the other rein is there to catch his nose, so he brings it down where it belongs, turning with his body straight, and his head steady.

Both these methods can be used in handling the reins. **The first method should be used when the horse is being worked fast, and the squaw rein when he is being worked slowly.** After he is further along he can be worked fast with the squaw rein.

The rider should not try to neck rein as it is not a sign of a well-trained horse at this stage. The way the horse handles himself at this stage shows how well-trained he is. He has to be handled so that he does not go out of position .

The rider must become adept at changing hands on the reins whichever side he is turning on, and automatically knowing where to take hold of them.

The use of the squaw rein comes easy with practice. The following illustrations show the two methods of handling the reins. **(See Figure 41.)**

If the rider is using the fast set and turn, and the horse stops and comes back smoothly, he will not have to work him against the obstacle any more, but can work him in the open. The rider can also stop the horse straight without turning, **but he must remember to put the dwell back in the reins, or the horse will bounce.**

The idea of the obstacle is to shorten the stop and teach the horse to turn correctly at the start.

The rider should never try to stop straight or make the horse slide if going real fast, or he will lose the sensitivity on the reins and will not feel the pull. This will spoil his slide.

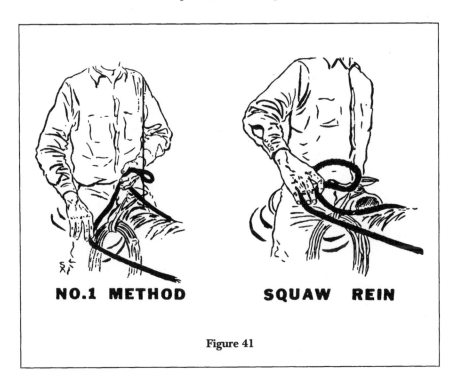

NO.1 METHOD   SQUAW   REIN

Figure 41

The rider should know automatically at what speed the horse will go and yet still try to set down and slide.

If the horse is going very fast and the rider wants to stop him quickly, he should pull one rein several times with a heavy enough pull that will check him, and pull straight back without doubling him. If the horse does not want to be checked on one rein, then the rider should double him. The horse should never be set straight unless he feels the pull. Use one rein and double him, if necessary. Then he will not get hard on the hackamore. **He must be kept light.**

Now the horse should be worked on animals against a fence. The best place to work him is in a square corral large enough so as to give him a pretty good run, and with smooth ground so there will be nothing to catch his feet.

Head the animal against the fence, and stay out from the animal far enough so as to always head him. If too close to the animal the horse will try to crowd instead of heading it.

The horse must always be handled so that he works according to the requirements of this kind of training. He must always be given time to work on his hind feet, and do things right at all times now.

After the rider heads an animal a few times he could get the animal in a corner, then let the horse hold him there by himself and help him a little with the reins. This should not be done too much at one time, or the horse will lose interest.

Horses like to play this way, but they should never be soured on it. A little bit now and then and they will get very good at it.

If done too much they will want to work too fast, and will not stop as they should. They will lose the sensitivity in the reins and get hard on the hackamore. When they get to working too fast, the rider should always make them wait for the rein, and make them work slow. Whenever they are worked either fast or slow they are worked so that they do things right at all times.

When practicing the spin the rider holds the rein out to the side where the horse can see the hand and with the angle to the hand that will bring the horse back on his hind feet as he turns. His hind feet have to be far enough under him so he can be on a balance. **(See Figure 42.)**

As the rein is worked with the pull and slack, the rider can hurry him up with the movement of his body as he turns. At the

Figure 42

start the horse may not make full half turns, but as long as he is coming off the ground with his front feet and turning on his hind feet a little he is doing all right. When he makes one complete turn, or three half turns, he should be jumped out at the same time so he does not go out of position. The rider can wake him up as he starts the spin by giving him a little tap with something on the hind leg opposite the side he is turning on.

The spin must not be overdone. If he turns half way properly he will turn all the way with a little practice. The rider must remember that he cannot teach a horse everything in a day. After the horse gets to know how to spin for three half turns, he will not have to be jumped out anymore. Jumping him out helps to keep him in position at the start.

Horses should be given long, slow rides now and then, but the hackamore should be looser than usual. The hackamore should always be as loose as possible and still have the horse give to it. The hackamore could be looser than usual when he is not being worked fast. The hackamore should never be cinched down tight all the time.

Practically all horses as they go along will try to get hard on the hackamore or will try to take their heads away from the rider once in awhile. They have to be handled so they do not get the best of him. Especially is this true of short, stubby-necked horses. The rider has to be able to double them to keep them in line.

When short, stubby-necked horses set their necks they are hard to double, and if they are able to take their heads away they will be able to run away. If they do not actually run away, they will still not be working true, or as light as they should. Then, too, they will learn to stick whenever they feel like it.

The best thing to use is the thong through their mouths, and up over the wraps of the hackamore, tied snugly. Work the horse easily and let him know what it is before pulling if possible. If

Figure 43

96

the horse is getting the best of the rider by pulling on the hackamore, the rider should pull him. As soon as the horse comes around on both sides leave him alone. **Do not pull him any more unless it is necessary.**

The rider can leave the thong on him for a few days if he thinks that he may have some trouble with him. As soon as the horse gives to the hackamore again, the thong can be taken off.

There are riders who can double any kind of a horse and there are a lot of them who can't. The ones who can't have to take the easy way to do it. There is a knack to doubling. It isn't the power, but the way it is done.

If a horse is trying to run away and the rider can't pull him, he should get a good hold of the rein on the side he is going to pull on, then bring his spur on the other foot up his belly, and pull hard at the same time. This will loosen up his neck for an instant so the rider can double him. **(See Figure 43.)**

When horses try to get hard on the hackamore it does not last long if they never get the best of the rider. The rider should use good judgment, never getting the horse on the fight if he can avoid it, as they will remember it a long time. Horses like these should be put in a snaffle bit until they get over their bull-headed ways.

Horses that cannot always be doubled will blow up on the rider sooner or later.

The rider should always keep in mind how to pull with the pull and slack. If he pulls steadily on the rein, he will be pitting his strength against the horse. He can't do that and win.

THE SPIN WITH THE SET AND TURN

When a horse is able to turn around on his hind feet for one complete turn, or three half turns, and is doing it pretty well, he can be worked at the spin with the set and turn.

A couple of times is enough at one time and **not every time he is ridden.** It is better to work him against an obstacle the first few times; pick a place where there is smooth ground so there will be nothing on the ground to catch his feet when he is set up.

If some of the horses are sliders the rider could wet the ground to make it more slippery; this will help them to slide.

If they are fast set and turn horses, it is not necessary to wet the ground, **but it should be smooth. (See Figure 44.)**

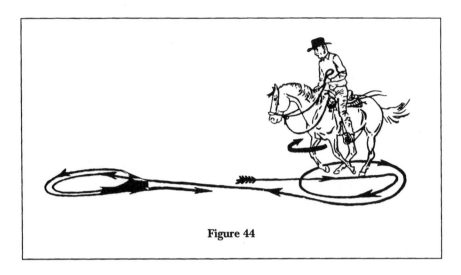

Figure 44

The rider could use No. 1 Method at the start. Run them down the obstacle, but not too fast, and set them up. If the horses are sliders the rider should put the dwell in the reins and pull one rein shorter than the other.

After the dwell, as the horse's front feet are about ready to touch the ground after the first half turn, the rider should feel him out on one rein, and as his front feet touch the ground, give him another light pull to turn again, and as his front feet touch the ground, give him another light pull to turn again. When he gets around far enough so that he can jump out on the last half turn facing back the way he came, give him a scare so he will jump out fast.

This is done on one rein; the No. 1, and the Squaw rein, is one rein. Do not try to throw the horses around with both reins, or they will get to lugging on the hackamore, and go out of position. It is always a light pull and slack and no heavier than his head.

HANDLING THE REINS

The rider could use both the No. 1 Method, and the Squaw rein if he wanted to, or he could use the No. 1 Method for fast work, and the Squaw rein for slower work.

With both of them the rider should watch head position by remembering what makes their noses fly up.

This is the same procedure as the set and turn, only he is making three half turns instead of one half turn and is going back the way he came all the time.

If the horses are fast set and turn horses, there will be no dwell in the reins, just the slack in the reins between pulls or movements. The turning, or spinning, is the same on all of them.

When they get so they can spin for three half turns they can be spun without jumping out, but the rider must be careful not to spin them so long that they will want to stick.

A string of horses should be pretty well positioned this far along. It should be remembered that the way the reins are handled keeps them in position at all times.

The rein is pulled straight back to the rider's stomach to stop, and is never pulled on steadily, either lightly, or heavily, or the horse will bore into the hackamore.

The rider is giving the horse a chance to stay in position as he works him. Keeping the horse in position puts the form to his work.

For instance, if the horse was standing still, and the rider had to turn him quickly, if he gave him one touch to turn, the horse would maybe come up too high off the ground with his front feet and would be unable to make a complete turn in a hurry, because his hind feet would be in the wrong place. If the rider gave him several light touches to get started, he would be able to turn properly, although it would not be so fast a turn as he would ordinarily make if he were ready for it, but he would be turning correctly.

If the horse was being worked fast, he could be picked up and turned fast because he would be ready for it. **(See Figure 45.)**

The rider is always changing hands on the reins whichever side he is turning on. Do not get in a hurry, as the horse improves slowly and gradually.

The horse should not be neck reined, or he will lose the form and class to his work by going out of position. Neck reining is for the **finished** product.

If the nose starts to go up, tuck him with a squaw rein as he goes along, with both reins in one hand with the slack in the long rein. Change sides once in a while.

When the nose goes up at this stage, it is because in the majority of cases, the rider is pulling too hard and steadily on the reins.

Figure 45

Remember: **do not double them too much at this stage.** The more they are doubled now, the harder they will get on the hackamore.

If the horse gets a little hard on one side, tuck him with pulls hard enough for him to feel. **(See Figure 46.)**

If a horse gets hard at this stage, and does not lighten up as he should, put a wide thong through his mouth and up over the wraps of the hackamore. Run him down the obstacle at a good fast clip, then reach down and get him on one rein, giving him one big hard pull and slack. Then back on the other side and do the same thing. Doing this will not injure him in any way. The idea of this is to scare the horse into lightening up. Sometimes a horse can be scared into doing certain things that he would not do otherwise.

Remember that the majority of horses will take advantage of a rider if they can, and a rider never likes to have a horse get the best of him. A hard hackamore horse cannot be worked properly.

Figure 46

If doubling the horse with the thong in his mouth does not scare him into lightening up, then the rider should use a hair hackamore on him for several days until he lightens up again. Then he should be put back in the regular hackamore again.

The horse has to be light in order for the rider to get the action out of him when he is being worked.

When a rider is on a balance he can time and pick the horse, thereby giving the horse a chance to get his feet in the right place all the time. The rider catches him in the air to stop, so he can shoot his hind feet under him in one movement.

Many riders at this stage will get in a hurry and start to work their horses at an advanced stage before they are ready for it; then the horse will go back on them. The horse will always show if he is ready for advanced work.

As the horses improve, they can be worked a little faster all the time in proportion to their improvement.

When working cattle always turn the horse on the same side the animal is on even if he turns so late that he loses the animal. This keeps the horse watching the animal all the time.

When the horse first goes into a bunch of cattle to part out, or cut, it should be in the open instead of a corral. In the open there will be many places for an animal to come out of the bunch, and in the corral there is only the gate. In the corral the horse would have to work faster than he is able to at this time and it may do him more damage than good.

After the horse puts an animal out of the bunch, the rider should make him stand for a few seconds and let him look at the animal he has just put out, so he can see what he is doing.

TAKING IN THE REINS

Taking in the reins should not be done until the horses are working with their feet in position. They do not have to be working very fast, but just so they can stop and turn right on the single rein. The same procedure of handling the reins is applied until they are all ready for the bridle. The only difference is taking the reins in from the wide Squaw rein, or the No. 1 Method, to where they can be neck reined straight up and still do things correctly. The wide rein, both methods, keeps the horse in position. When taking the reins in, do it gradually so the horse will not go out of position. **Gradually means a few months.**

Some horses will take to it right away, but for the average run of horses, it has to be done little by little.

With both methods of handling the reins, the long rein keeps the horse turning with his body straight, and the touch and slack is done on a loose rein.

The rider should not press the rein over the horse's neck to try to teach him to neck rein, as this will eliminate the touch and turn, and throw his feet out of position. The horse will be able to be picked up and put any place with a light touch and slack after awhile.

With the No. 1 Method when one rein is pulled the other catches his nose and brings it down; the fingers should pull on the rein in order to feel out the nose. The little finger and the one next to it should do the pulling. The long rein takes care of itself with the touch and slack firmly fixed in the rider's mind.

The fingers of each hand are used with the Squaw rein. As the reins are worked, the short rein, or the rein on the side the horse is turning on, will be on the outside of the hand at the little finger.

As the horse is turned the little finger and the one next to it will do the light pulling with the movement of the hand.

Both reins will go between the thumb and the finger next to it. The fingers of each hand will separate the reins. The long rein between the thumb and the finger next to it will slip according to how wide the rider is working the reins, and the finger next to the thumb regulates the long rein.

A rider can feel out a horse's nose better by using the fingers on the reins, and if the horse is light, and he should be, the fingers are all that it will take.

The same procedure is practiced at all times while taking in the reins until the horse is ready for the double reins.

Now to take in the reins: the wide rein (both methods) is gradually narrowed down until the horse is practically working on the neck rein straight up. And he is kept in position.

A good working horse may, however, go out of position after the reins have been taken in a little. He should then be worked with a wide rein again to bring him back in position by steadying his head so he will throw his hind feet into position.

When working the horse fast while taking in the reins, go back to a wide rein so he will keep his feet in the right place.

As the horse improves, he will get to work truer all the time and become less liable to get his feet in the wrong place. Then he can be worked faster all the time.

Once in awhile all horses will try to get lazy, and try to do things half way; the rider should wake them up with a sting or two, and make them work; if they know how to work they will.

The horse should work when the rider wants him to, not when the horse wants to. The rider should be the boss at all times.

The rider should not keep his horses on their toes all the time. When there is no need to wake them, let them alone.

After the reins have been taken in to where the horses are practically neck reining straight up, the rider should keep changing hands on the reins on the side he is turning on.

Every now and then, circle the horses and wind them up in a spin, always jumping them out, and circling the other way without stopping from the spin.

The rider should give his horses practice at the spin with the set and turn once in awhile, and also just the spin.

No part of the training should be overdone from now on. For example, **the less the rider slides his horses now the better they will slide.**

In other words, the rider should not be pecking at his horses all the time. When it is time for them to work, make them work, then let them alone.

Many riders, after they get their horses working well, will overdo them just because they do work well. **This is the time to take it easy with them.**

When they work true all the time with the reins taken in, then it is time to start them in the double reins. They do not have to be neck reining straight up before they are started in the double reins; the rider always works one rein a little shorter than the other until the horse is ready to be worked on the bit a little. **(See Figure 47.)**

Whenever a horse has been turned out for any length of time, he will be off in his work for a few days or a week.

A rider should not work, or run horses on a hackamore horse as it will make him unmanageable, and hard on the hackamore. A good hackamore horse can be spoiled in a very short time doing this.

The details of handling light, medium-heavy, and heavy-headed horses have been given. Once a rider has a horse coming the right way, it is not hard to keep him that way, providing the rider has an idea of what to do next. May this information be of value to him.

A person is not born with all the knowledge he needs for any line of endeavor. He has to learn it, and it takes time to learn any business. With this training period it is important that the beginner gets the proper fundamentals of handling young horses, and a picture of the entire build up at the start. As time goes on he will keep on improving if he follows the game.

Figure 47

EPILOGUE

IN MEMORIUM
THE OLD TIME GREAT HORSE BREAKERS OF CALIFORNIA

The good ones stood out far above the others. They were in a class by themselves. They are gone but not forgotten.

Even in the old horse days, the good ones were few and far between. They consisted not only of Spanish Californians but men of any nationality who had reached the top. They followed through with the original concept of the California-reined horse.

The finished hackamore and bridle horses they produced were incomparable. It was a physical impossibility for those horses to work any better. They would work a cow, and they worked to perfection on the rein. The men who reached their peak from the early 1900's up until the 1930's were the last of the great California horse breakers.

The growth of California spelled the end of a way of life that had been handed down from the days of the Spanish Dons. The land had become too valuable just to run cattle. The immense land and cattle companies turned to intensified farming. The cattle had become a side issue.

Slowly and gradually, the range passed out of the picture. With the development of the land, and as mechanization came to the fore, the great horse breaker of California passed into oblivion, but he faded out easily.

It is better for him that he is not here now, or he would be lost.

Ed Connell